A CHEERFUL BOOK OF MISFORTUNES

A CHEERFUL BOOK
OF MISFORTUNES

Ean Wood

Book Guild Publishing
Sussex, England

First published in Great Britain in 2010 by
The Book Guild Ltd
Pavilion View
19 New Road
Brighton, BN1 1UF

Illustrations by Mike Bastin

Typesetting in Garamond by
Ellipsis Books Limited, Glasgow

Printed in Great Britain by
CPI Antony Rowe

A catalogue record for this book is available from
The British Library

ISBN 978 1 84624 529 9

Man is born unto trouble, as the sparks fly upward.
— Job 5: 7

Meditate upon exile, torture, wars, diseases, shipwreck, so that you may not be a novice to any misfortune.
— Seneca

By trying we can easily learn to endure adversity. Another man's, I mean.
— Mark Twain

In spite of all that has been said for and against God, it must be admitted even by his severest critics that he has a sense of humour.
— Eric Temple Bell

Contents

Introduction

Life is full of surprises, some of them disconcerting. This is true even for someone as grave and wise as myself. I have spent long years pondering on the human condition, often when I should have been doing something else. I have pondered on steep and rugged Scottish mountainsides and in the welcoming doorways of Soho, both places prone to producing interesting surprises. But my most recent (and disconcerting) surprise came on reading through this book, collected over half a lifetime. I intended it to be a useful and instructive guide to life's pitfalls, a book that would help people learn through the misfortunes of others. Alas, it has turned out to be nothing of the sort.

How much use is it, for instance, to most of us, to learn to beware of burying dead lighthouse-keepers in solid rock, to watch out for falling cherubs, or to refrain from playing the violin on roller-skates? Or to learn that a corpse cannot be removed during a live TV show? And how much use is it to the man in the street to tell him to watch out for leaping elephants if his ship is sinking?

No, I am afraid the book is a failure. All it can hope

to do is amuse, surprise and touch the heart. It is a good job I am humble, or I would be much disheartened.

Humbly I offer my readers these short tales of real life, feeling confident they will be encouraged by the failures of others, as most of us are.

Ean Wood

1

Home Life

It is often pointed out that the domestic environment offers the most danger – that most accidents happen in or around the home – the bare wire, the falling chimney-pot, the skateboard on the landing. And around the home the most dangerous place of all is bed (over 93 per cent of over-70s die in bed). But even out of bed, home life in all its safe warm protectiveness can be bloody dangerous. And in the long and unhappy list of domestic accidents, some, by their very unexpectedness, carry a flavour all their own. For instance . . .

In Johannesburg in 1970, a man and his wife had recently moved into a new house. Not long after they moved, they were in bed when the burglar alarm went off. No doubt cursing somewhat, the man hurried to investigate. But not yet being used to the house, he ran into and smashed a glass partition separating the lounge from the dining-room. His wife called an ambulance, and he was taken to hospital to have his lacerations attended to.

While he was gone, his wife set to work cleaning up his bloodstains. Finding that water was not too effective, she tried using sheets of petrol-soaked kitchen-roll. Having used them, she threw them into the bowl of the toilet.

Her husband returned, stitched and bandaged, and went to the toilet. Sitting there, he lit a cigar. After the resulting explosion and sheet of flame, his wife called the ambulance again. This time, one of the ambulance men, carrying him out on a stretcher in the dark, tripped over the edge of the rockery in the garden. The husband, tipped to the ground, broke his collar-bone. And there had been no burglar.

Hulbert Taft Jr was well-connected and successful. His grandfather had been a half-brother of President Taft, and he was chairman of the Taft Broadcasting Company, which owned sixteen radio and TV stations, and the programmes it produced included *Huckleberry Hound* and *The Flintstones*. Born in 1907, he lived with his wife and grown-up family (a son and two daughters) on a rich estate in Indian Hill, a suburb of Cincinnati.

But in spite of his success he was worried about The Bomb. There was an old wooden house on his estate, about 300 yards from the main house, and he worried to such an extent that in 1959 he had a private bomb-shelter built under it, for himself and his family. It was a sizeable shelter. Inside, it measured 40 feet by 70 feet, and it was stocked with all the usual provisions and equipment for a long stay – tinned food, bottled water, reading matter, bottled gas for heating and cooking, an electric generator, and so on.

For eight years nothing happened. Then, in 1967, he went there alone to make a regular inspection. While he was in there, the shelter exploded. Bottled gas had been leaking, and something – a cigarette, a light-switch, the generator – ignited it. If he hadn't worried so much he might still be alive today.

The Collyer Brothers were eccentric, to say the least. They were born in New York, Homer, the elder, in 1881, and Langley, the younger, in 1885. In 1909 their father, a doctor, bought a big five-storey house at 2078 Fifth Avenue, in Harlem. Harlem had been developed in a hurry in the 1880s when speculators decided the New York subway system would soon reach the area. Big wide streets were built, and hundreds of expensive houses and high-rent apartments. Unfortunately, the rich and respectable proved in no hurry to move so far uptown, and in the 1900s the speculators, to recoup their losses, began renting and selling to well-to-do Black people. Hence the growth of Harlem as a thriving Black community. Dr Collyer and his family were something of exceptions.

Homer and Langley, unlike many white Americans of the time, did not suffer from racial prejudice, and after their parents died they continued to live in the same house. Homer was slightly the more assertive of the two, which is not saying much because Langley was definitely timid. His real interest in life was classical music, and he was talented on both piano and violin. Both became admiralty lawyers, but when Homer went blind in the Twenties and had to retire, Langley gratefully retired too.

They had plenty of money to live on, and for the next twenty years or so became totally reclusive, although Langley would on rare occasions sit on his front steps, wearing sneakers, and chat to passing Harlem residents. He rarely left the house, except to buy food (mostly they lived on buns and peanut butter) and to rummage in skips or garbage cans. He became a great collector, especially of newspapers and magazines, which he would read to Homer and then hoard, so that Homer could read them himself when he regained his sight. They were both convinced that this would happen, and to this end Homer ate endless oranges, sometimes a hundred in a week. 'They will cure his blindness,' Langley once said. 'Remember, we are the sons of a doctor.'

Gradually the whole house became filled with stuff collected by Langley. Rooms and landings were crammed to the ceiling – so full that the only way through many of them was through narrow winding passageways that were all the space that was left.

Then, owning so much stuff, they began to worry about burglars. So Langley constructed many booby-traps in the passageways between their possessions – tripwires or perilous piles of tin cans to bring tons of bales and boxes tumbling down on intruders.

In March 1947 neighbours became concerned that the house was even more quiet than usual. With some difficulty, the police forced their way in. Making their way cautiously through the winding passageways, they found the body of blind Homer Collyer in a room on the second floor, clad in a tattered grey bathrobe. He had been dead for at least two weeks.

The question was, where was Langley? After waiting a couple of days in case he showed up, the police put out an eleven-state alarm to trace him. They also began searching the cluttered house, tunnelling in through the basement and through holes they made in the roof.

They found thousands of old newspapers. They found magazines and cardboard boxes and broken furniture. This had possibly been collected as fuel – there were also dead tree limbs, some of them seven feet long and twenty inches in diameter.

There were eight crates of ledgers, and legal documents. There was a mahogany cabinet crammed with dirt-encrusted dishes and chinaware. In bookcases in the basement library there were over 2,500 books, many on medicine, mechanics and the sea. There were old car parts, the folding top of a horse-drawn carriage, and thousands of empty bottles and cans.

There were umbrellas and hats and three dressmaker's dummies, and several pin-up girls, dating from around 1910. There were old rusted bicycles and gas chandeliers, and many toys and weapons. There was a horse's jawbone, and a box of old campaign buttons, with such half-forgotten slogans as 'Win with Wilson' and 'Vote No on Women's Suffrage'.

As every schoolboy knows, this sort of obsessive hoarding is now believed to result from a physical deterioration of the frontal lobes of the cortex of the brain. But that is merely the explanation. It takes nothing from the scale and splendour of Langley's achievement.

Most of what he had collected was quite worthless, but some was not. There were fourteen grand pianos (badly in need of maintenance), five violins, and a fake Stradivarius cello (wrapped in cloth and obviously well cared-for). All in all, 120 tons of stuff was ultimately removed. Cranes had to be used. Many Collyer cousins, none of whom had seen the brothers for years, showed up and forced the police to stop throwing rubbish away, claiming it might be valuable.

It says something about how much clutter there was that when the police did trace Langley, after eighteen days searching, he was in the house, in the same room as his dead brother, and only about ten feet from him (although under four feet of rubbish). He was in a passageway only two feet wide, between a chest of drawers on one side and an old bedspring on the other, and he'd died from being caught in one of his own booby-traps, suffocated under a mound of debris, while carrying food to his brother. As a result, blind Homer had starved to death.

Charles Kingsley, author of *The Water Babies*, was a Christian clergyman with a tendency towards both mysticism and healthy Victorian good-sportsmanship. He adored his wife, Fanny, but always believed he would outlive her, and when, in late 1874, she fell ill with heart trouble, he sat for hour after hour in her icy December bedroom, planning with her every last detail of her funeral. As a result, he caught bronchitis, and was himself confined to bed. As it happened, their beds were at opposite ends of the rectory they lived in, and for a month they were able to communicate only by sending notes to each other. Then, in January, it was Kingsley himself who died. One small consolation is that, being a devout believer, he had always awaited his own death with 'reverent curiosity'. Fanny outlived him by twenty years.

Professor John Tyndall, FRS, born in humble circumstances in Ireland, became in Victorian times a pillar of the British scientific community. A colleague of Faraday and Huxley, an Alpinist, and a great populariser of science, he was the first man to work out why the sky looks blue.

He was also hot-tempered and contentious, falling out with a number of colleagues and fellow-climbers (he angrily resigned from the Alpine Club when fellow-member Leslie Stephen, father of Virginia Woolf, made fun of earnest Victorian climbers who, even after hair-raising climbs, would give a justifying scientific aspect to their activities by, for instance, measuring the air temperature and pressure).

He was also apparently a born bachelor, so it was a surprise to many when, in 1876, he married Louisa Charlotte Hamilton, especially so as he was 56 and she was only 31. Nonetheless, theirs turned out to be an ideally happy marriage, loving and tender. As someone said of them, 'They were companions in all things.'

Around 1890, when he was 70, Professor Tyndall's health became poor. He began taking a few drops of chloral hydrate at night to help him sleep, and magnesia in the morning for his digestion. The bottles of these stood beside his bed, and were usually administered by Louisa. On the morning of 4 December 1893, however, a new bottle of chloral had arrived and been placed beside the others, and at 8.30, by mistake, she gave him a whole spoonful of it.

Tyndall said, 'There is a curious sweet taste.' Louisa looked at the bottle and said, 'John, I have given you chloral.' To which he gently replied, in one of the saddest phrases ever uttered, 'Yes, my poor darling, you have killed your John.'

She had. In spite of all their efforts, and the efforts of doctors, which included emetics, strong coffee, and the stomach pump, he gradually sank into unconsciousness and, at around 6.30 in the evening, died.

Louisa survived him for 47 years, dying in 1940, aged 95.

In the mid 1980s, an American housewife, living on an isolated farm, sensibly bought herself a large chest-freezer. Once it was installed, she proudly called a friend on CB radio to tell her. She hadn't yet bought half enough provisions to fill the freezer, so she had done the energy-saving thing, and as she told her friend, 'At the moment it's full of bags of grass.' Within minutes the whole house was surrounded by police-cars with flashing lights and blaring sirens. Monitoring CB radio transmissions, they had got the wrong idea.

2

Our Dumb Friends

For centuries animals were regarded as inferior beings, but to those among us who love the furry, the hairy, the scaly, the spiky and the slimy, it seems they are just as intelligent as many people. They can even do things that humans cannot – pigeons can navigate amazingly, bloodhounds can follow a scent, gibbons can swing from branch to branch with an elegance that would put Olympic athletes to shame. Hens have such a strong maternal instinct that they will try to hatch a china egg. But just sometimes even non-human creatures, obeying their brute instincts, behave in ways that can only be described as dumb.

Elizabeth Magill, aged 16, of Holbrook, New Jersey, was walking her dog on a summer day in 1977. The dog was on a metal leash, and he stopped, as dogs will, to urinate. Unfortunately the spot he chose was an electrically-illuminated sign outside the Holbrook Medical Center. Current passed up his stream of urine, through him, up the metal leash, and into Elizabeth, knocking her unconscious. He was killed.

On a December morning in 1869, two young men named Bellis and Jones decided to go rowing on the Mersey, near Tranmere. Bellis had with him his faithful dog, and they were some way from shore when their small boat capsized, tipping all three into the water. Jones was a good swimmer, but Bellis could hardly swim at all. Jones naturally made efforts to save him. But the faithful dog scrambled up onto his struggling master's back, and every time Jones came near it bit him, snarling and growling, and drove him off. Bellis drowned.

In a case of gamekeeper turned poacher, Andrew Thornton, who had been a narcotics agent with the police in Lexington, Kentucky, decided he would himself engage in a little drug-smuggling. Before his time with the police he had been a US Army paratrooper, so nothing seemed simpler. Flying to South America in 1985, he purchased 79 lb of pure cocaine, worth an estimated 13 million dollars. He packed it into two army-issue duffel bags, equipped himself with food, night-vision goggles, two knives and some ropes, and attempted to evade customs by re-entering the country by parachute. But his parachute failed to open fully, and Fred Myers, who lived near Knoxville, Tennessee, was somewhat surprised next morning to look out of his window and see Thornton's body lying in his back yard. His duffel bags were not with him.

Some weeks later, in the neighbouring state of Georgia, a man hunting in the Chattahoochee National Forest found one of the bags. It had been torn open, and beside it were the bones and hide that were all that was left of a bear, dead of a six-million-dollar overdose.

Mark Platt, aged 19, of San Diego, California, had a pet female python. One day in 1979 he was sitting watching TV with all ten feet of her curled up on his lap when suddenly it entered her head to clamp her jaws round his genitals. Unable to persuade her to release her grip, he was eventually forced to phone the emergency services. It finally took 15 firemen, 3 ambulance crews, 2 policemen and an animal control expert to free him, after ninety minutes of extreme discomfort. A useful hint for anyone who finds himself in this unfortunate situation is that they did it by giving her a quick whiff of smelling salts.

3

The Official Mind

It is easy to laugh at bureaucrats – at administrators, account-ants and general paper-shufflers – at those whose only hope of plugging in to the great current of human life is to record and codify it, who feel they can face life confidently only when equipped with facts and figures. Among them of course being those in posts of authority, such as ticket-inspectors, tax-collectors, and local government officials. But without such administrators where would the more disorganised among us be? Singing the summer through, maybe, but starving in the frozen foodless winter. So it's grossly unfair to mock them. After all, they are human. Which is no doubt why from time to time they behave like prats.

It was a fine spring day in 1907 at Felling, near Gateshead. After a frosty night, it had become surpris-ingly hot and sunny. So hot, in fact, that the sun had heated the rails in a cutting enough for them to buckle from expansion. A man crossing a bridge over the cutting noticed this, and at once went to the driver of a steam-roller working not far away. He explained the situation to him.

The driver, seeing that the rails had become like 'an elongated letter S', at once ran as fast as he could along the top edge of the cutting to a nearby signal-box and advised the signalman to stop any approaching trains by putting his signals to 'Danger'.

The signalman was less than co-operative. He asked, 'Who are you and what has twisted the rails?' 'I can't say,' said the steam-roller driver, 'but if you don't stop the train it will be a bad job.'

The signalman didn't stop the next train, travelling from Leeds to Newcastle, and it was a bad job. The engine and most of the carriages were derailed. Eight passengers were gravely injured and two of them later died.

Rune Lindquist was deputy fire chief in the old Swedish village of Varnhem. In 1979, a farmer in the village had an old wooden barn that he wanted pulled down, and a demolition firm had quoted him a sum equivalent to £445 to do the job. Lindquist, hearing of this, had a bright idea. He suggested to the farmer that if the shed was set on fire, putting it out would give his part-time firemen valuable practice. They would make sure that when they were done the shed would be completely destroyed, and they would charge the farmer only half of what the demolition firm quoted.

The farmer agreed, and early on 21 May Lindquist poured two cans of petrol into the barn and put a match to it. Soon it was blazing fiercely and, fanned by strong winds, the flames soon spread to other buildings, none of them in any particular need of demolition. Twenty hours later, other fire brigades, hurriedly called from surrounding areas, were still helping to extinguish the blaze. Twenty-one buildings in all were destroyed, including shops and houses. Five families were made homeless. A villager was reported as describing Lindquist and the local brigade as 'bloody amateurs'. Which seems quite mild, really.

The 1994 football World Cup was to be held in America. The police of the town of Gilroy, in California, not too familiar with professional soccer but aware of the dangers of hooliganism, decided to hold a practice exercise.

Theodore Brassinger, a police reservist, was detailed to act as a hooligan. Indulging in a simulated act of vandalism on Gilroy station, he was so convincing that he was shot dead by a colleague.

The 1920s in fashionable Germany were a time of hectic sensation-seeking. In Stuttgart, a polar bear belonging to a circus died, and the owners offered it as an unusual meat to the proprietor of a fashionable restaurant, Der Königsbau. The proprietor, being a conscientious and law-abiding German, phoned the local food inspector for permission before buying the animal.

The equally conscientous and law-abiding food inspector duly consulted his rule-book and solemnly assured the proprietor that polar bears were not mentioned in it. Therefore there would be no need to provide the inspectorate with samples of the meat for analysis.

The proprietor bought the dead bear, and its meat duly appeared on the restaurant menu as 'Eisbärenschinken' (polar bear ham). As a result, eighteen people, including the proprietor (who had tried it) came down with trichinosis – a serious infestation with the larvae of a parasitic worm more usually caught by the less fashionable from tainted pork.

With the Sixties still in full swing, Norman Fuchs, the Mayor of the little mining town of Zap, North Dakota, encouraged students from North Dakota State University in their plan to descend on his town on Friday, 9 May 1969 for a Mother's Day 'Zap-Out' ('Zap' was a with-it word in those days, and became the title of a hugely influential underground comic). Mayor Fuchs imagined several hundred peaceful hippy students playing music and having a few drinks, and thought it would be good for business. He went round wearing a T-shirt which read 'Zap N.D. or bust!'

The town's population, however, was only 300, and some 2,500 students turned up, nine-tenths of them male. They found too little to do and, becoming drunk and bored, they began smashing windows and scattering merchandise.

Later, as evening fell and the day became cold, they felt the need for warmth. So they tore down and made a bonfire of tavern partitions and tables, and the whole of an empty frame building. A car approaching the bonfire was attacked and wrecked, as was the volunteer fire-truck, attempting to control the bonfire. Ugly fist-fights started.

Mayor Fuchs, whose dream of a small boom for his town had collapsed, was observed wandering along Main Street in a daze, muttering, 'Animals! Animals!' In desperation he phoned the State Governor, who sent in five hundred armed men of the National Guard.

Eventually the students were gone, but not one of the town's four stores was in a fit condition to open for business next day, and most were severely out of pocket.

Victor Biaka-Boda was a member of the French Senate. He represented the Ivory Coast, in West Africa, which was then a protectorate of France. Remembered by colleagues as a 'small, thin, worried-looking man', he set off in January 1950 to visit the hinterlands of the country he represented, and to investigate those things that were causing his constituents concern. Among these was known to be a food shortage. They ate him.

On an isolated small island in the Bahamas there used to be a shipping beacon called Double-headed Shot Light. It was administered by Britain's Imperial Lighthouse Service and was tended by several keepers in rotation. Each keeper took his tour of duty alone, but there was sufficient accommodation on the island for his family, if he should wish it. In 1928, one such keeper, in residence with his family, suddenly died.

This presented his family with a problem. No relief was expected for several days and, the weather being warm, it soon became desirable to bury him. But the island was composed entirely of solid rock, so digging a grave was impossible. They did, however, find a natural cavity in the rock. It was narrow and vertical, but the only possible place. So they lowered his body into it upright, and placed a heavy boulder over the cavity to close it.

As they stood round conducting an improvised funeral service, a violent storm blew up. They finished, and were leaving the site when suddenly they heard a loud report. The cavity, unknown to them, was a blow-hole connecting like a chimney to a cave at sea-level, and, as a wave pounded into the cave, they turned to see the corpse shoot headfirst into the sky like a rocket.

The whole thing was considerably distressing, and when the Imperial Lighthouse Service learned of the matter they acted in true bureaucratic manner. They sent labourers to build four concrete graves – two for adults, two for children – each with a heavy concrete lid. But Double-headed Shot Light was decommissioned before they were ever used.

In 1926, an open-air fete, organised by the Conservative Party, was being held in the village of Market Bosworth, in Leicestershire. It was while a woman was reciting the poem 'Waiting for something to happen', that a wooden bridge collapsed and fifty people fell into an old moat.

4

Of Course It'll Work

Engineers, technicians, scientists, and such fauna are, of course, among the cream of humanity. When you think of all the things that man has tried over the years and found out don't work – like sprinkling water on stones to bring on rain, or holding the head of a live frog in the mouth to ward off thrush – it's amazing how many things clever researchers have found over the centuries that really do. Every invention that makes life easier or safer or more rewarding is due to them, from artists' colours and musicians' instruments to lighthouses and non-stick underwear. So let it not be assumed, when I set down the following reports from the field, that I view the misfortunes of some as hinting at the folly of many. Man must strive, and why should we be surprised if now and then a wonderful new idea turns out a bit funny.

The Kemper Arena, in Kansas City, was a notable piece of public architecture. In 1979 it was awarded a prize by the American Institute of Architects, who called it 'one of the finest buildings in the nation'. The members of the Insititute were so impressed that, soon after awarding the prize, they went out of their way to hold their annual conference near it. On the first day of the conference, hordes of architects toured it, admiring the great span of the metal roof trusses, described in *The Architectural Record* as having 'an almost awesome muscularity'.

Next day, without anyone near it, it collapsed in a tangle of metal and masonry.

François Reichelt was a young tailor working in the suburbs of Paris. These were the early days of aviation, and the idea of parachutes as a safety device had been much discussed. Reichelt was inspired by this to manufacture a special one-piece safety suit for airmen. It was an elaborate contraption of a baggy tweed, with batlike wings between the arms and sides, and a further great bag of tweed behind him, supported by a tall frame of flimsy metal tubes.

To publicise his invention, he decided to make a jump, wearing it, from the first storey of the Eiffel Tower. The proprietors of the Tower were not keen, but reluctantly said they'd give him permission if he also got authorisation from the police, and if he signed a waiver absolving them of all responsibility. The police agreed, he signed the waiver, and on the cold morning of 4 February 1912, wearing his bat suit, he took his position on the edge of the first storey, 60 metres above the ground.

A newsreel crew was alongside him to film his jump, and when he hesitated, suddenly not sure that this was a good idea, they urged him on. He did jump, and fell to his death like a stone, becoming the first man to die through media influence. The film exists.

One of the most bizarre disasters of all time occurred on 15 January 1919, in Boston, Massachusetts. A cylindrical storage tank, made of half-inch steel plates riveted together, stood in the area called the North End, near the inner harbour. Looming over the freight-loading depots, it was 58 feet high and 90 feet in diameter, and contained over 14,000 tons of raw black molasses. It belonged to the Purity Distilling Company, and just after noon, while the only company employee on the site was off having lunch, its lowest ring of plates burst, the rivets popping like gunfire.

Investigations, which, as so often, took years, eventually established that possibly fermentation had built up pressure in the tank, but that in any case it was built of thinner steel than had been specified in the plans.

As soon as it burst, a moving wall of molasses, some 15-feet high, swept down Commercial Street and into the waterfront area, pouring through the streets at an initial speed of 35 mph and sweeping away everything in its path. Neither pedestrians nor horse-drawn wagons could outrun it. Passers-by, wading into the flood to help others, were themselves trapped. Fourteen buildings were smashed. A firehouse was pushed off its foundations and almost swept into the harbour. The girders supporting an elevated railway collapsed, and a train approaching the collapse was halted just in time. A professional boxer, asleep in a third-floor room, awoke in several feet of molasses, which it turned out had drowned his mother downstairs.

Eleven people in all were drowned or suffocated, and sixty were injured. Horses trapped in the gooey tide had to be shot by the police. For weeks fire hoses and pumps laboured to empty cellars. The harbour ran brown for months, and the smell of molasses lingered in the area for years.

Louis Slotin, one of the young scientists who worked at Los Alamos on the development of the atomic bomb, was the man who worked out by experiment what was the critical mass of uranium – the lowest mass at which a lump of it would spontaneously explode in a nuclear reaction. This had to be done experimentally. To work it out theoretically would require impossibly complex calculations.

A key experiment was to slip two hemispheres of uranium onto a rod, and slide them gradually towards each other, measuring the radiation given off. Slotin habitually did this using two screwdrivers, a fiendishly dangerous practice that he positively enjoyed, calling it 'twisting the dragon's tail'.

It was on 21 May 1946, some months after the Second World War was over, that he was employing this technique while watched by seven colleagues. Suddenly one of his screwdrivers slipped. The hemispheres moved too close together and the whole room was filled with a dazzling bluish glare. Effectively what Slotin had in front of him was a live atomic bomb, but bravely and instantly he grabbed the hemispheres with his bare hands and wrenched them apart.

Then he realised that this near-disaster might provide valuable information about the effects of radiation. Telling his colleagues go back to where they were when the accident happened, he sketched their relative positions on a blackboard. Then he and the colleague who, next to himself had been closest to the uranium, went to wait by the roadside to wait for a car to take them to hospital for examination. As they waited, Slotin said quietly to the colleague, 'You'll come through all right. But I haven't the faintest chance myself.'

He was right. He never left the hospital, and died nine days later.

Reuben Tice, aged 68, who lived in Monterey, California, and ran an electrical shop, was not only a skilled engineer, but was also well known as a spare-time inventor. Among other things, he had successfully invented a device to chill cocktail glasses, and a system of electrical underfloor heating.

California is famous for its prunes (among other things), and it occurred to Reuben that it was a pity they were so wrinkled in appearance, making them look somewhat unappetising. So he began working on a device to correct this.

His proposed method involved subjecting prunes to extremely low pressure, and in November 1967, while he was testing his prototype device, it imploded. A part of it, a metal cylinder ten inches long and with several valves attached, struck him on the head and killed him instantly. When his body was found, the half pound of prunes scattered around him were as wrinkled as ever.

At the beginning of the Twentieth Century, Prosper Blondlot was a reputable French scientist at the University of Nancy. It was at a time when one of the most exciting new discoveries was X-rays, and many scientists were investigating whether there might not be other similar rays that were previously undetected.

Working in his laboratory, Blondlot believed he had discovered such rays. They could be refracted through a prism – not a glass prism, such as refracts light, but one of aluminium – and they could be detected by minute, almost invisible, deflections of a galvanometer needle. Proudly, he named them N (for 'Nancy') rays. Scores of learned papers describing their properties appeared in French journals, and the French Academy offered Blondlot a prize for his discovery.

Then, on the evening of 21 September 1904, the American scientist Robert W. Wood visited Blondlot at his lab. He had been sceptical about N-rays, believing that the needle deflections Blondlot thought he was observing were so small that they might be caused by self-deception. While Blondlot was bent over his apparatus, observing and describing the N-ray spectrum, Wood slyly removed the important aluminium prism from the apparatus. Blondlot continued to observe and describe.

Wood's subsequent paper describing the event (although

not naming names) effectively destroyed poor Blondlot, who could never bring himself to admit he had been mistaken.

It was 1980, and prospectors working for Texaco, searching for oil, were drilling into the bed of Lake Peigneur, in Louisiana. Unfortunately they did not know that beneath it was a disused salt-mine. When their drill broke into the mine, the lake swiftly drained away, sucking down five houses, nine barges, eight tugboats, two oil-rigs, a mobile home, most of a botanical garden, and a substantial area of nearby Jefferson Island. The crater left was half a mile wide.

John Day, an eighteenth-century Suffolk wagon-maker, was once described as 'gloomy, reserved and peevish'. Whether or not that was true, he was certainly desperate to achieve fame and fortune. His opportunity came when an idea struck him whereby a man might survive underwater. It was simplicity itself. All that was necessary was to construct an absolutely watertight box.

He bought a small decrepit fishing-boat, built such a compartment inside, took it to a large pond near Yarmouth, got in, and had the boat weighted with boulders till it sank. He stayed on the bottom, thirty feet down, for a while (he said twenty-four hours, but you don't have to believe everything), then he released the boulders by tugging on a rope and the boat floated to the surface.

'Elated with success', he now set about to capitalise on his idea. Needing funding, he wrote to a well-known gambler and man-about-town of the day, named Christopher Blake. If Blake would put up the money, he (John Day) would build a bigger and better version, and they could make money by wagering that he would stay underwater for an unbelievable time.

Blake accepted without hesitation. He advanced Day £350 to build a new 'diving box', and would give him ten per cent of all he won from betting on his survival.

Going to Plymouth, Day bought an old fifty-ton sloop, the *Maria*. He again constructed a watertight compartment, and placed seventy-five empty hogsheads inside it for added buoyancy. He packed ten tons of ballast in the hold, and a further twenty tons was slung beneath the keel by means of ropes. This, as before, could be released from inside his watertight compartment when he wished to return to the surface. He then painted the *Maria* bright red, and announced that he would descend in her to 50 fathoms (300 feet) and stay there for 24 hours.

Blake hurriedly talked him into amending this to 20 fathoms for 12 hours, and started laying odds. On 20 June 1774, the *Maria* was towed out of Plymouth harbour while a brass band played and the crowd cheered. Blake passed among them, taking last-minute bets.

In Plymouth Sound, the *Maria* was sunk 22 fathoms deep. Day, inside the box, had a bed, a watch, a taper, some biscuits, and a bottle of water. He had planned to release coloured floats from time to time during his descent, but he never did. Nor did he ever surface again. Rescuers tried to grapple the boat and raise it, but with no success.

What John Day had failed to take into account was the pressure that water exerts at depth. When 22 fathoms down, which is 132 feet, his box would have been subjected to a pressure of more than 60 pounds per square inch, and the likelihood is that it broke up long before he ever reached the bottom. Nonetheless, he did earn the celebrity he had wanted, being the first man ever to lose his life in a submarine disaster. Christopher Blake, quickly fearing that Day had not survived, vanished with the stake money. It seemed to him the best thing to do.

5

Trust Me, I'm a Doctor

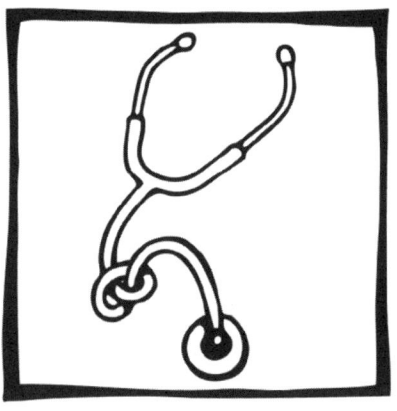

Medicine is a great and noble calling. Unfortunately, it seems to call to some people with a muffled and indistinct voice. I do not mention such therapeutical disasters as pre-frontal lobotomy, goat-gland transplants (sorry, Yeats), or the Victorian crusade against self-abuse (a term now rather misunderstood – in 2005 The Guardian, in its obituary of a famous tenor-player somewhat given to introducing substances into himself, described him as having died after 'a lifetime of self-abuse'). Nor do I speak of such famous names in the field of medicine as Crippen, Palmer, Pritchard or Shipman. I speak only of those of purer intentions, and their misfortunes. And besides the misfortunes of doctors, there are also the misfortunes of others in the make-it-well sector. For instance . . .

In the 1920s Monsieur Desmalles was a patient in a nursing-home in Paris. For him, the chief physician prescribed the ingredients for a lotion, for external use only. His clerk wrote out the prescription, mistakenly entering it on a form for internal medicines.

In due course the form came to the dispenser who was to make it up. He confused two drugs, and mixed into the lotion one that was poisonous.

The head pharmacist, who was supposed to check all prescriptions, was busy, so he left the checking to his assistant. She failed to do so.

Another assistant, knowing there was another patient in the home called 'Desnoyelles', and thinking the name 'Desmalles' on the label was an error, 'corrected' it to

'Desnoyelles', then passed the bottle on to the houseman who was to administer it to the patient.

The houseman, disregarding the stated dose on the label, simply handed it to Monsieur Desnoyelles and told him to 'take a good big swig'. Monsieur Desnoyelles did.

Not long afterwards he died, the victim of one of the longest known chains of human error.

On New Year's Day in 1886, in his home in Pimlico, Edwin Bartlett was found dead in bed with a stomach full of chloroform. Doctors were baffled. How could such a large dose of such a corrosive chemical have possibly got into his stomach, whether accidentally or on purpose? His attractive wife Adelaide was accused of his murder, tried, and found not guilty. After which Sir James Paget, the surgeon to Queen Victoria, is said to have remarked, 'Now she's acquitted, she should tell us, in the interests of science, how she did it.'

Adelaide herself was ten years younger than her husband. She was bored and unhappy, and having an affair with a neighbouring Wesleyan minister (with Edwin's approval). And she is something of a mystery. Of unknown parentage, no-one was sure where she came from, and after her trial she disappeared without trace.

Crime-writer Raymond Chandler's theory was that Edwin, who was addicted to patent medicines, had a digestion like a goat's, and probably thought he was drinking ginger-ale.

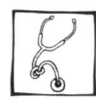

Elisha Perkins, described by one of his biographers as a 'celebrity par excellence in the quack line', was born in 1741, the son of an eminent doctor in Norwich, Connecticut. Himself having studied medicine, possibly at Yale, he set up in practice in Plainfield, also in Connecticut. Electric healing was much in vogue at the time (there being an idea in the air that electricity was in some way connected with the 'life force'), and enthusiastically he followed the fashion. In 1796 he invented what he called 'Perkins's Metallic Tractors', which were a sort of metal tongs, supposed to draw out aches and pains from the body.

These he manufactured and sold himself (at $10 per pair), becoming both famous and wealthy. Until, in 1799, a British doctor published an article entitled *Imagination in Healing*, revealing that he had achieved results just as good using a pair of wooden tongs. Perkins's vogue was over, and at around the same time he was expelled from the Connecticut Medical Society for being 'a patentee and user of nostrums'.

Unbowed, he persevered with his cures and invented a sort of cure-all tonic, which was simply a combination of vinegar and muriate of soda (an old technical name for common salt). Among other things, he announced it as a new and infallible cure for yellow fever (which at that time was raging). There was an outbreak of it in New York and, seeking to re-establish his great reputation, Perkins went there to administer his tonic. Possibly he even believed it would work but, after four ineffective weeks, he caught yellow fever himself, and died. Even quacks can be unlucky.

The brothers Thomas and Arthur Allbutt were consultant physicians working in Leeds in the late nineteenth century. Thomas later went on to fame and fortune and a knighthood, but in 1887 Arthur wrote and had published a helpful little book on childcare. Its title was *The Wife's Handbook*, and unfortunately for him it contained a concluding chapter on contraception. Eminently sensible by today's standards, it poured scorn on some of the useless ideas then in vogue, instead suggesting such reasonably reliable methods as using 'French letters' and douching after sex.

Fellow-members of the medical profession were horrified that he would openly publish such things, shedding a slimy light on the seamy side of life. Their outrage caused the General Medical Council to hold a special (and secret) meeting, and at the meeting what seemed to upset them more than anything was the possibility that the book might be perused by unmarried persons. This possibility also used to worry the great Charles Darwin, who had died only five years before – he feared that knowledge of birth control might destroy chastity (a fear we now know to have been unfounded). Arthur was struck off the Medical Register and his career ruined.

Mary Mallon was Irish-American. Whether she was born in the USA or emigrated there was never established. Nor was her exact age, although she claimed to have been born in 1870. Mary had a tendency to be cagy.

Striking in appearance, she was of medium height, with a build that would have been athletic if she was not just the slightest bit overweight. With blonde hair, sparkling blue eyes, and a determined set to her jaw, she was a forthright, even pugnacious, woman, and not enormously bright (why do those last two qualities so often seem to go together?). This made it many times more unfortunate that she was a carrier of typhoid – a carrier being someone who is highly infectious themselves while remaining immune to the disease they incubate. This was a concept Mary would prove entirely unable to grasp, so it was even more unfortunate that her only way of earning a living was as a cook.

She was an excellent cook, although somewhat sloppy in such cleanly matters as washing her hands (which was part of the problem), and in a day when many households employed a cook she had no difficulty finding work.

It was in August 1906 that she first came to public attention, when cases of typhoid occurred in the seaside resort of Oyster Bay. Many New Yorkers spent the summer there, and it was for the summer that she had been hired, by a wealthy banker, General William Henry Warren.

There were eleven people living in his rented house, and six of them got the disease. But by the time typhoid expert Dr George A. Soper arrived there to investigate,

Mary had gone. Tracing her career back through various employment agencies, he suspected that during the past six years twenty-six people had caught the disease from her, in seven separate outbreaks ranging all over New England.

It took him four long months to track her down, cooking for a family in a big old-fashioned house on the western side of New York's Park Avenue. There, a laundress had been taken ill with typhoid, and a daughter of the family was actually dying of it. Meeting Mary at last, and interviewing her in the kitchen, he found she would tell him nothing of her past career, and angrily denied ever having typhoid in her life. When he asked if she would agree to undergo tests, she said nothing, but simply picked up a carving fork and advanced on him. Dr Soper fled.

Mary also fled, but this time Dr Soper found her more quickly. She was now working in a rooming-house. Soper, this time prudently accompanied by an assistant, waited for her in the kitchen. Arriving and seeing him, she became incandescent with fury, and soon the two men left, pursued by a volley of curses.

This time Soper swiftly called in the law. Three policemen and a woman doctor went to the rooming-house. Mary ran from them and hid in an outside toilet belonging to the house next door. But they found her and, after a struggle, arrested her. By now she was nationally known as 'Typhoid Mary'. Hospital tests established definitely that she was a carrier, and she was imprisoned in an isolation centre at North Brother Island.

From there she kept up a vigorous campaign, appealing

to the courts for her release, and suing the authorities for $50,000 damages. Neither suit succeeded, but after three years, in 1910, she did get parole, on condition that she report regularly to the Board of Health and never take employment as a cook.

Mary had an answer for that. She cooked under a succession of assumed names. Using such aliases as Marie Bresshof and Mrs Brown, she began working at a succession of sanitariums and hospitals, causing a succession of small outbreaks, and leaving in a hurry. The worst, at the Sloane Maternity Hospital, caused 25 cases, of which two died.

Eventually she was tracked down working for a family in Westchester County, and this time was sent to North Brother Island to stay. There she lived on until her death in 1938, strongly protesting the injustice at first, but gradually subsiding into a resigned acceptance. From later investigations, it seemed likely that she had caused the great 1903 outbreak in Ithaca, New York, where there were over 1,300 typhoid cases. But as Mary would have said, how could that be when she had never had the disease in her life?

In 1888, Charles McLane, aged 22, entered the Roosevelt Hospital in New York City to be operated on for an abscess on his hip. He was given ether as an anaesthetic, and the abscess was successfully removed. Then, still unconscious, he was placed on a trolley.

The operating theatre was on the first floor of the hospital, and an orderly, Herbert Bennett, wheeled him to the lift to take him up to his ward. The lift was rather a primitive affair. To operate it, the single door had to be opened and a rope pulled to operate a hydraulic valve, bringing the lift either up or down.

Unfortunately, another orderly had opened the door to find out where the lift was, and then hurried off to wheel a patient into the waiting theatre. Bennett, seeing the door open, assumed the lift was already there, and without thinking wheeled the trolley into the empty shaft.

As the trolley's wheels went over the edge, McLane began to slip off it. Bennett grabbed for him, but managed only to retrieve the trolley. McLane fell two floors to the basement, landing on his head. He died an hour later, never waking.

6

Arms and the Man

Of course when it comes to misadventures with firearms, America leads the world. When I was young my father, who sold and repaired firearms, subscribed to "American Rifleman", the journal of the gun-toting National Rifle Association. In every monthly issue there was a column called "The Armed Citizen", which with solemn glee recounted recent news items in which ordinary Americans, mostly small storeholders, had killed or gravely wounded petty criminals. Needless to say, at the age of nine these exciting tales filled me with shocked delight. I felt that owning a real live gun must be a wonderful thing. But guns are unpredictable machines, and not only in America.

In 1921 a Sussex man, named Bonham, was walking around his home town of Haywards Heath, when he saw smoke rising in the distance. Heading towards the smoke, he discovered it was his own house on fire, and on hurrying there also discovered that the fire had been caused by his 11-year-old son using paraffin to start a bonfire (children will do these things).

Helped by neighbours, he began removing from the burning house as many household goods as he could. Then he stood outside, taking a breather for a moment. Unfortunately, he had not got round to removing a particular bureau. In this bureau he kept a loaded revolver. When the flames reached it, a shot rang out, and Bonham clutched his chest, staggered a few steps, and fell dead.

By appalling bad luck his own revolver had shot him through the heart.

One evening in 1971 Kenneth F. Ballew, of Silver Spring, Maryland, was in his bath and his wife was in her underwear getting ready for bed, when their apartment door was burst open by a battering ram and six bearded men rushed in.

Mrs Ballew screamed to her husband to get a gun (he was a keen collector, and owned over twenty of various ages and calibres). Naked and dripping, he rushed to obey, but it was too late. One of the men shot him in the left lobe of the brain, paralysing him for life. 'Murder!' Mrs Ballew screamed. 'Get the police! Police! Police!' But the raiders, there by mistake, were the police.

The date was 2 August 1876, and the place was Deadwood City, Dakota. In the No. 10 Saloon, on Main Street, James Butler 'Wild Bill' Hickok, sat down to play poker with three friends – Captain Massey, Carl Mann and Charlie Reid. For a joke, they decided to keep Wild Bill out of his usual seat, with his back to the wall (the safest place for such a notorious gunman). He protested, but Massey, who had the seat, refused to move, and eventually Wild Bill took the chair opposite him.

As they were playing, a young man named Jack McCall, ambitious to be known as a gunfighter, entered and shot Wild Bill in the back of the head. The bullet, passing through, entered Massey's forearm. Massey immediately jumped up and ran out into the street, yelling (in alarmed confusion), 'Wild Bill shot me!'

This caused something of a panic in the town, but soon it was discovered that Wild Bill himself was dead. He had died instantly, his hand still crimped to hold his cards, a pair of aces and a pair of eights – a hand known to poker-players for ever after as the dead man's hand. (The fifth card, for those interested, was a queen.)

Of all the six bullets in McCall's revolver, it turned out that only the one that killed Wild Bill was not a dud.

In the days of the Wild West it was unusual for women to involve themselves in gunplay. But at the Olympic Gardens, Denver, in 1877, this did happen. Mattie Silks, the town's leading madam, was giving a champagne party for the cream of the local whores. After the party had lasted some time, and many involved were well lubricated, Mattie got the idea that a fellow-madam, Katie Fulton, was making a play for her man, Corteze 'Cort' Thompson. Accusations and denials flew, and it was decided that the matter could only be decided by a duel.

Cort Thompson, proud to have two fine women fighting over him, agreed to act as referee. Mattie and Katie stood back to back, with loaded pistols, and on his command each took three paces, turned and fired. They missed each other, but a shot from one of them severely wounded Thompson in the neck. He was very much annoyed.

Terry Kath was the lead singer of the highly-successful American band Chicago. In early 1978, when the band had been together for ten years, and he was 33, he attended a party at the Los Angeles home of Don Johnson, a member of the road crew. Everybody, including Kath, had a few drinks and a pleasant time, and eventually the party broke up, leaving only Kath, his wife Camelia, and Johnson.

As they sat together, Kath, who was an enthusiastic target-shooter, as usual had on him a 9 mm automatic pistol. This he now pulled out and started twirling it round his trigger finger. The gun made Johnson nervous, and he asked Kath to stop playing about. 'Don't worry,' said Kath, 'it's not loaded. See.' He put the gun to his head and pulled the trigger. He'd been mistaken, but he never knew it.

Carl Kiger was a prominent member of the small city of Covington, Kentucky, being its Commissioner and Vice-Mayor. He and his wife, Bonnie, had four children. The eldest two were away on active service, for it was 1943

and America was at war, but their daughter, Jo Ann, aged 16, and their young son, aged 6, were with them at their luxurious summer home in Rosegate when, one night in August, Jo Ann had a nightmare. She dreamt that burglars had entered their home and were murdering her entire family. Maybe she got this idea because her father was obsessive about burglars. This was why he kept a number of loaded revolvers hidden about the house.

Still asleep, Jo Ann grabbed up a revolver and began roaming through the darkened house firing it at anyone she found. As time went on she picked up a second loaded revolver, then a third. She fired fifteen shots in all, killing her father and her young brother, and leaving her mother crippled by a shot through the hip and crying in bewildered pain.

Her rampage went on for an hour before she began to awaken. Half-awake, she returned to her badly-injured mother's room and said, 'There's a crazy man in here and he's going to kill all of us. I don't want to be left alone in here.'

Naturally her mother believed her, and it took some time for police and neighbours to piece together what had actually happened. When they did, Jo Ann was arrested on a charge of first degree murder. But her defence offered evidence that she had had previous nightmares, and that she was a confirmed somnambulist, and the prosecution could not produce a shred of motive. She was acquitted.

Mrs Laura Baines, of Penzance, in Cornwall, had a fine orchard, but was troubled by apple-thieves. So in 1959, to deal with this problem she hired a man to patrol the orchard at night with a gun. Which would have been fine except that she didn't trust him to do his job. So she crept out one night to check he was not asleep. He was not. He shot her dead.

7

The Game's the Thing

As a young man I was appalled by the apparent uselessness of sport. I could never understand why W.G. Grace was the world's most famous Englishman, or why C.B. Fry was offered the crown of Albania. But then I realised that its function is to provide good news in the media (sport apart, people don't much like cheerful news items – they'd much rather read about misfortunes). Then I also came to understand it as a force for world peace. Of course the early film director D.W. Griffith thought that by the year 2024 the same thing would be achieved by silent cinema, but sport enables nations to meet other nations as fellow human beings, and is a fairly amiable mock-war without much bloodshed, constraining competitive aggression into more-or-less civilised channels. Nonetheless, with so much energy being channelled, sometimes things do go wrong . . .

It was the day of the 1972 Windsor to Chiswick marathon. At the ten-mile mark, a policeman on duty held back the traffic, and kindly directed all 127 runners down the wrong road. It took marshals, police-cars and motorcyclists nearly an hour to round them all up again.

Kathy Ormsby was as perfect as a student could get. At high school in North Carolina she had a 99 per cent scholastic average, was class valedictorian, and a star of the running track. She broke state records in the 800 metres, the 1,600 metres and the 3,200 metres. In her senior year her school even held a special 'Kathy Ormsby Day' to honour her.

Going on to college at North Carolina State, having won both academic and athletic scholarships, her prowess continued. Majoring in pre-med, she also set a new inter-collegiate women's record in the 10,000 metres. Much of her success, she felt, she owed to her devout belief in God.

Less than six weeks after setting her intercollegiate record, she ran in her most important event of the year, again a 10,000 metres, in the 1986 NCAA Championships in Indianapolis. Competitors were there from all over the USA.

She got through the heats and into the final, and for the first 6,500 metres of the race all seemed to go well. She was in a group of four pulling away from the rest of the pack. Then things started to go wrong. The other three in the group started to pull away from her. For almost the first time in her life she was failing. She started to suffer the desperate feeling that (as she later said) she was letting down God, her coach, her teammates, and her parents.

Suddenly her mind snapped, in what psychiatrists call a panic attack. It was as if she was outside herself, just watching herself, no longer in control. When the leading runners reached the back curve and set off round it, she just kept straight on. She ran under a barrier, up the stands, across a baseball field, and over a chain-link fence seven feet high. Then she kept on running, harder, she said afterwards, than she had in the race, along busy New York Avenue.

About half a mile from the stadium, this avenue crosses a bridge over the White River. Reaching the bridge, Kathy climbed its guard rail and threw herself headfirst over it to land on a bank 35 feet below. On the way down, she later remembered, she apologised to God, saying she was sorry.

She survived, but broke a rib and her spine, thus becoming wheelchair-bound for life. But she announced plans to go back to North Carolina State and qualify to become either a minister or a medical missionary. As her father said, 'We have accepted this and have faith that somehow it will be used to glorify God.'

He also said, thoughtfully, 'I believe that it had something to do with the pressure that is put on young people to succeed.'

The 1971 Pan American Games were taking place at Cali, in Colombia. Angelo Rodrigues, aged 23, was in the habit of hanging round outside the athletics stadium. When he noticed a vehicle slowed by traffic, one with a conveniently open window, he would reach in, grab what valuables he could, and make his escape into a maze of back alleys.

A coach came along and was slowed down. Quickly he reached in and grabbed a tracksuit, a travel bag, and two cameras. Then, as usual, he fled. Unfortunately for him the coach was carrying the women's 100-metre sprint finalists. They chased him, caught him, and were very angry with him. He was turned over to the police with a torn shirt and bleeding hands.

The most famous early nineteenth-century mountaineering disaster happened on 20 August 1820, when a party organised by Dr Joseph Hamel, a Russian scientist, was making the final ascent towards the summit of Mont Blanc, the highest peak in the Alps. There were eleven of them – Dr Balmat, two Oxford students, and eight guides or porters. They were not roped together, and at one point were ascending a snow-slope lying at an angle of about thirty degrees. This snow was only about twelve hours old, and was crusted to a depth of about half an inch, with soft snow below. Suddenly the surface cracked right across, just above the line of men, and slid away downwards in an avalanche, carrying the whole party with it. It carried them at least 1,200 feet, to where there was a huge crevasse. Rushing into this, the snow took with it four of the guides, filling the crevasse to the brim and forming a heap more than forty feet high over the top of it. Incredibly, one guide was rescued, blue in the face from suffocation, but the other three were lost.

The crevasse was in the famous Boissons Glacier, and it was estimated by experts that its slow crawl downwards would cause the bodies of the three lost guides to appear at its foot, five miles away, around forty years later. Forty-one years later this did happen. The romantic story is that one of the surviving guides, now an old man of seventy, visited the foot of the glacier and once again set eyes on the companions of his youth, still looking as youthful as they had so many years before. In fact, however, the remains of the guides and their belongings were found thoroughly fragmented and strewn over a wide area, which is hardly surprising as their five-mile journey had taken them over at least one ice-fall. The fibres of one knapsack were strewn over an area of hundreds of square feet, and the bodies were similarly dispersed.

Charles R. Traub had been a cameraman for Pathé News for fifteen years. On 13 March 1929 he went to Daytona Beach, Florida, to film an attempt on the world land-speed record, being made by Lee Bible, driving the 'Triplex Special'. This monstrous and extraordinary car consisted of little but three Liberty aero-engines bolted onto a massive chassis and generating a total of 1,200 horse-power. Two of these engines, at the rear, were permanently coupled to the rear axle, and one, at the front, was coupled to it by a clutch. The vehicle was set in motion by starting the front engine only, then gently letting in the clutch, thus setting the rear axle in motion and letting it start the rear engines. The whole affair, totally devoid of streamlining, weighed about four tons and was described at the time as 'a combination of brute force and ignorance'.

Traub set up his camera just past the end of the measured mile, about 100 feet to the side of the course, saying to a fellow-reporter, 'If you want to see real action, you'll get it right here when that fellow takes his foot off the gas crossing the finishing line. At that speed, something is going to happen.'

He was absolutely correct. Travelling at over 200 mph, the inexperienced Bible, a garage-owner who had hardly ever driven a really fast car, and never one half so heavy, cut his motor too sharply. It swerved, then rolled over, breaking every bone in his body. Then it headed for Traub, cranking his silent camera. Traub cranked for as long as he dared, then abandoned the camera on its tripod, and ran. The 'Triplex Special' swerved again, caught him, and cut him in two. The camera, standing where he had fled from it, remained untouched and unharmed.

Joseph Merlin invented roller-skates. A Belgian instrument-maker, he had moved to London in 1760, and it was there that he made his famous effort to publicise them. Attending a masquerade ball, he made a striking entrance among the dancers – he swooped in on his skates, dressed as a minstrel, and playing a violin. Whizzing across the dance-floor, he crashed into a full-length mirror, smashing both it and the violin. For the time being, roller-skates were a failure.

8

That's Entertainment

Show-business is one of the great achievements of mankind. To create a perfect performance, with unbelievable (but often unobtrusive) skill, before an audience that wishes (indeed, hopes) to be hypnotised by magnificence, takes years of practise. Of course, solemn art-loving idiots have railed against it, protesting that it is lying and untrue – that, for instance, the wonderful and heart-lifting Lem Beasley was a miserable shit in private life, and thus his whole performance was a fraud (oddly, they never much say this about, say, Wagner or Rimbaud). But the sheer pressure of producing perfection, even in such pre-recorded forms as film and television, often creates unusual situations, such as do not occur in real life. This sows a fertile field for calamity.

In 1929 the director William Wellman, working for Paramount Studios, was filming *Wings*, set in the Great War. It was to be magnificent and spectacular and expensive. For a major scene a whole stretch of battlefield had been constructed, complete with trenches and shell-craters, and the whole set had been planted with mines to provide realistic explosions. There were hundreds of actors and extras, and many airplanes (Wellman himself claimed to have flown in the war with the famous Lafayette Escadrille – that unit of Americans fighting in the French Air Force before America entered the war). There were also many cameras, to cover the action from all angles.

Wellman was directing operations from a railed platform on a hundred-foot tower, from where he was planning to give the signal for 'Action' by waving a red flag (this was before the days of public-address systems, and the set was so big that a megaphone would be inadequate). On the platform with him were his First Assistant Director and one of the Cameramen.

Jesse Lasky, overall head of production at Paramount, joined them there, fresh from Hollywood. Wellman boasted a little about the scale of the scene, telling Lasky, 'When I wave this red flag, you'll see $60,000 go up in smoke' (a considerable amount in 1929). Then he decended from the tower to make some last-minute adjustments. A little later Lasky learned that the mayor of the local town had arrived, by invitation, to watch the spectacle. Courteously he sent word inviting the mayor to join him on the platform. The mayor was glad to do so and arrived, accompanied by his 13-year-old daughter.

Lasky found him a canvas-back chair, and told him and his daughter as much as he could about the impressive preparations. Then conversation flagged. The preparations, as is the way on even small film set-ups, were taking a long time. The mayor's daughter, becoming bored, looked around over the platform's railing, watching the activity below and the gathering crowd.

Suddenly she saw a schoolfriend there. 'Yoo-hoo!' she called. 'Mildred!' She shouted several times, but the noise from below was too great for her friend to hear her. Her eye fell on the red flag. Still shouting, 'Mildred! Mildred!' she snatched it up and waved it.

All hell broke loose. The mines began exploding in sequence, and the army of extras charged this way and that, as planned, through the ensuing clouds of smoke.

Planes, taken by surprise, roared into the air in criss-cross confusion. Only the cameramen, expecting more notice, were not ready. Not a foot of film was shot, and the $60,000 did go up in smoke. It took Wellman's crew several days to rebuild the battlefield.

In February 1951 the Spike Jones Band began appearing in *The Colgate Comedy Hour*, on America's NBC television channel. This frantic and often hilarious band was then at the height of its popularity, and every week the whole show was performed by it and its members, with various guests. The theme was Variety, so as well as musical numbers and songs, the shows included short sketches, many of them skits on such things as sporting events or movies.

In those days there was no video-recording, so the shows, transmitted from New York, had to go out live. And because they had so much crazy speed and diversity, it was decided that the sets should be mounted on a revolving stage, so that new ones could be set up out-of-sight as the performance went along.

On Sunday, 16 September, things went badly wrong. First, the revolving stage stuck. Then a master electrician rushed to try and correct the fault and fell dead of a heart-attack over the switches. As Spike himself recalled: 'The rest of the show was complete chaos. To top the whole thing off, in New York City there is a law that you can't move the corpse until the coroner has examined the body. So, here in the middle of an English drama or a baseball sketch, or Helen [Grayco] singing a song . . . were cops, priests, coroners and everyone that would be concerned with a man dying, walking past in front of the cameras and through all the scenery.'

And all of it went out live.

On 7 July 1972, Tom Pretty, a mechanic, was working in the back yard of his home at Queensborough, Leicestershire, on a gun intended for firing a human cannonball a hundred feet. In the course of his work he crawled down the barrel, and was making some adjustments there when he felt a massive blast of air round his head as the gun accidentally went off. It hurled him thirty feet, and over a wall. Worse, he landed on a live electric cattle-fence.

30 October 1939 was a Sunday, and every Sunday CBS Radio in America broadcast a play by the Mercury Theatre, directed by the 23-year-old Orson Welles. As a Halloween spoof, they decided to present a dramatised version of H.G. Wells' novel, *The War of the Worlds*. They presented it in documentary style, as if Martians actually were invading the world, having landed in a space-craft near Grovers Mill in New Jersey. Oddly, in view of what was

to happen, many involved in the production feared it was one of their poorer shows – that the style was unconvincing and that Martians were old hat. It was nearly replaced by *Lorna Doone*.

Radio was then the most popular and influential medium in America, and millions were listening. The forty-minute programme began at 8 pm, and many listeners, believing the story to be true, panicked. In Newark, New Jersey, in a single block, more than twenty families rushed out of their houses with wet towels or handkerchiefs over their faces, and this was typical of hundreds of thousands of others.

In the parlor churches of Harlem, evening services became emotional 'end of the world' prayer meetings. In Rhode Island, weeping and hysterical women swamped the switchboard of the *Providence Journal*, desperate for details of the massacre, and officials of the electric light company received a score of calls urging them to turn off all the lights so the city would be safe from the enemy. *The Boston Globe* received a call from a woman 'who could see the fire'. A man in Pittsburgh hurried home and found his wife in the bathroom with a bottle of poison in her hand screaming, 'I'd rather die this way than that!' (fortunately he was able to prevent her).

In a Southeastern women's college the girls in the sorority houses and dormitories huddled round the radio, trembling and weeping in each other's arms. They separated themselves from their friends only long enough to take their turns at the telephones to make long-distance calls to their parents, saying goodbye for what they thought might be the last time. In Minneapolis a woman ran into a church screaming, 'New York is destroyed, this is the end of the world! You might as well go home to die, I just heard it on the radio!'

Apparently, by the end of the show many people had either fled or were too stunned to hear Orson Welles sign off with a chuckle, saying, 'If your doorbell rings and nobody's there, that was no Martian . . . it's Halloween.'

By then the radio station was under siege, both physically and by phone. The mayor of a Midwestern city, for instance, phoned in anger to report mobs in his streets, women and children huddled in churches, violence and looting, and if this is a joke he's coming to punch Orson Welles on the nose. Reporters demanded to know how many deaths had been reported, what about the fatal stampede in a Jersey hall, what about the suicides?

As it turned out, in spite of the mass panic, there were no deaths and only one reported injury – a young woman who fell and broke her arm fleeing downstairs. The nation shamefacedly resumed its normal life, and Orson Welles became famous.

What is little-reported is that ten years later a radio station in Quito, the capital of Ecuador, broadcast a similar adaptation of the same story. Most Ecuadorians had presumably never heard about the Welles broadcast, and there was a similar panic. Only this time an angry mob poured petrol into the building housing the station and burned it down. Six of those involved in the show were killed, along with nine others.

The Great Lafayette was a fine and famous illusionist. Born in Munich in 1871, the son of a Jewish silk merchant and jeweller, at the age of 19 he had been taken by his father to America, where he entered vaudeville as a quick-change impersonator who did a little conjuring. He turned out a better illusionist than conjuror, and by the time he came to Britain in 1900 he was at the head of his profession.

He was a small, dapper man, and a martinet to his company, who, among other things, all had to raise their hats to him in the street and be strictly teetotal. A bachelor, he lived alone in a big house in London's Tavistock Square. With no human companion, his entire affection, to a morbid extent, was lavished on his dog, Beauty. She had been given to him in America in 1899 by the great Houdini, and travelled everywhere with him, staying in his hotel suites and having a suite of her own in his house.

His illusions were ingenious and baffling. Typical was one in which, playing the part of an artist, wearing a long cape and a beret, he had before him an assistant standing in a frame. Using wigs, beards and other props, he would make the assistant up as personalities of the day, such as Edward VII or Lloyd George, and ending with Tsar Nicholas II of Russia. At the end, as the Tsar stepped out of the frame to approach the footlights, Lafayette would walk off into the wings and, at the instant he disappeared, the Tsar would remove his beard and wig to reveal himself as none other than – Lafayette.

Many were also spectacular. His big finish, entitled 'The Lion's Bride', involved thirty principals and supers, and took place in a Pasha's harem, with incense burning, gorgeous hangings, and many electric lanterns and lighting effects. At its climax, when Lafayette, playing a Persian officer, had disguised himself as his own sweetheart, wearing a yashmak, in order to save her from the wicked Pasha, he would be bundled by guards into the cage of a lion (a real lion). The lion would roar and leap, then tear off its head to reveal, again, Lafayette.

On 9 May 1911, during a run at the Empire Palace Theatre in Edinburgh, disaster struck. Shortly after 11pm, Lafayette was just about to tear off his lion's head when a ball of fire was seen to fall from the flies, setting alight some of the hangings. Probably it was caused by a short circuit in one of the lanterns. None of the scenery was fireproofed, and soon the whole stage was ablaze. Cast and crew ran for their lives.

The drop curtain, upstage of the iron safety curtain, was hastily lowered, followed by the safety curtain itself. But that stuck thirty inches from the floor. A door at the back of the stage had been opened, and wind had blown the drop curtain forward, fouling the safety curtain. Smoke and flames billowed out under it towards the auditorium, over the heads of the orchestra, who were frantically playing 'God Save the King' in an attempt to avoid a panic.

Fortunately there were enough exits for the audience of three thousand to escape through them in three minutes, although some people got a little bruised. Backstage it was different. In an attempt to protect his trade secrets, Lafayette had ordered that three of the five backstage exits should be kept locked, and a fourth was barricaded by scenery. Although the Edinburgh fire brigade had the fire out by 12.15, ten cast and crew lost their lives. Lafayette was among them, as were a horse he rode in 'The Lion's Bride' and the lion itself.

Two days later his body was taken to Glasgow and cremated. Then, that evening, came his last illusion. A body, undoubtedly his, from the rings it wore, was found under debris in the theatre basement. The man that had been cremated in error was Charles Richards, a double he used in many of his illusions.

It was believed that Lafayette had run to the basement to try and rescue the horse. He in turn was hastily cremated at Glasgow, and his ashes were buried in Piershill Cemetery, Edinburgh, in an urn between the paws of the embalmed Beauty. She had died of apoplexy five days before he did and, grief-stricken, he had been forced to buy the Piershill plot for himself so that she could be decently buried there.

In the early 1860s an out-of-work American actor, proud of his ability with make-up, disguised himself as President Lincoln to attend an audition. He didn't get the part and, worse, on his way home, still in costume, he was assassinated.

9

Up in the Air

Flying through the air is of course an unnatural thing for man to attempt. But somehow we've managed to concoct a number of ways (Dr Johnson famously laid down that now we'd discovered the balloon that was quite enough – we could fly, OK, and now he'd rather find a cure for asthma). Flying isn't easy, and god knows it needs a lot of atmosphere-polluting fuel, but at least it's safe. Per passenger-miles travelled it's the safest form of mechanical transport there is, apart from possibly space-travel. All the same, it takes only a moment's inattention for the whole enterprise to become ill-advised. Or even a moment's idiocy . . .

Early one autumn morning in 1947 an American Airlines C-54 set off from Dallas, en route to Los Angeles, with a first scheduled stop at Phoenix, Arizona. It was a four-engined, propellor-driven aircraft, carrying 48 passengers and with a crew of five. Of the three in the cockpit, all with the rank of captain, the senior, and the man in charge of the plane, was Captain Charles Sisto. But he was not at the controls, he was sitting in a jump-seat behind the other two. In the co-pilot's seat was Captain Melvin Logan, and beside him, acting as pilot, was Captain John Beck, who had the least experience of the three and was piloting in order to get the feel of a C-54.

At about 550 miles from Dallas the plane passed over El Paso. It was at a height of 8,000 feet, and all seemed well. Then Captain Beck, at the controls, felt it mysteriously begin to climb. Unknown to him, Captain Sisto, sitting behind him, had for a joke moved a control called the gust lock, which was intended for use in turbulent weather, and had the effect of locking the rear elevators.

Captain Beck moved the controls a little towards 'nose down' to counteract the climb. This seemed to have no effect, so he moved them further. Still this had no effect.

Puzzled, he asked Captain Sisto if the automatic pilot was on. Captain Sisto assured him it wasn't and, realising that Captain Beck would soon catch on, suddenly flipped the gust lock off, expecting that the plane would suddenly dip, giving Captain Beck a surprise, and perhaps a slight scare.

Unfortunately, the controls had been moved further than he realised. The plane dived suddenly into an outside loop and ended flying back towards Dallas, upside-down. Almost everybody in the plane fell to the roof, including Sisto and Beck. Only one person didn't, and fortunately that was co-pilot Logan, who alone had his seat-belt fastened. As the plane fell, he managed to get it under control just before it hit the ground. It was then at 400 feet, and thus had fallen over 7,500 feet. Fearing damage, the crew immediately turned back and landed at El Paso.

The period upside-down was described variously by passengers as 'a split second' and 'an eternity'. Fortunately, though they were shaken and bruised, none of them was seriously injured. And the plane turned out to have sustained only minor damage 'as a result of the unusual manœuvres and strain placed on the structure, and by the occupants striking the lining of the cabin'. American Airlines announced Captain Sisto's resignation.

Tom Attridge, formerly a pilot for the US Navy, was a test pilot for the Grumman Aircraft Engineering Company, of Bethpage, Long Island. On 21 September 1956, he was testing an F-11-F1, a new single-seater jet fighter, designed to operate from an aircraft-carrier. Flying at a height of around 13,000 feet, and at the supersonic speed of 880 mph, he was off Long Island and entered a shallow dive in order to test the plane's four 20 mm cannon by firing non-explosive practice shells into the Atlantic.

He fired a four-second burst (some 60-odd shells), then entered a steeper dive and fired a second similar burst. At the end of the second dive his windscreen was suddenly shattered. At first he thought he had hit a bird, and headed at once back to base. But on the way there his engine went dead, and he was forced to crash-land half a mile short of his field. The plane was badly damaged, and he broke a leg and three vertebrae.

It turned out he had caught up with the shells he had fired himself, thus becoming one of the few pilots ever to shoot himself down.

At the start of one of the most foolish air accidents of all time, a BOAC Hermes airliner set off on a scheduled flight across North Africa from Tripoli to Lagos, carrying eight crew and ten passengers. The date was 25 May

1952, they set off at around 2am, and they were to fly a little over 1,800 miles.

In the cockpit were the Captain, the Co-Pilot, and the Navigator. Unfortunately, they all seem to have been poor at navigation. Both Captain and Navigator did hold second-class navigator's licences, but the Captain had been awarded his only after his third attempt, and the Navigator had barely scraped through to get his after his fifth.

Their first mistake was to incorrectly set their gyro-compass. It had a variation control on it, to trim it into accuracy, which should have been set at three degrees west, gradually rising to six during the flight. The Navigator set theirs to thirty degrees west, gradually rising to sixty. Thus as soon as they set off they were well off course.

Noticing a discrepancy between the gyrocompass and the plane's magnetic compass, the Captain asked the Navigator to take a 'star shot' to confirm their bearing. He took several, but failed to notice that he was aligning his sextant on the wrong star. He told the Captain that the magnetic compass must be faulty, and the Captain pronounced it 'unserviceable'. At this point the cockpit crew would have been well advised to fly back to Tripoli, but instead they decided to carry on. Nor did they attempt to radio any nearby airfields, to get a check on their bearing.

A little later, after they had been flying for a couple of hours, the Co-Pilot noticed the incorrect setting on the gyrocompass, and pointed it out. It was corrected, and the gyrocompass now agreed with the magnetic compass. But by now they weren't at all sure where they were.

An hour or so later, at around 6am, they began sending out SOS calls. But for a while the airfields that might have picked them up – Gao, Niamey, Kano or Tessalit – were too busy chatting to each other to do so. They were discussing what might have happened to that Hermes.

After quarter of an hour they did get replies, from Kano (in Nigeria) and Accra (in Ghana), both many miles to their south-east. Accra took over. The Captain had by now decided that the best airfield to head for would be Port Etienne, on the west coat of northern Africa, in what is now Mauritania, so Accra gave the crew instructions for getting there. But everyone failed to take into account that the plane no longer had enough fuel to reach Port Etienne.

It eventually ran out of fuel and crash-landed in the soft sand of the Sahara Desert, 150 miles from Port Etienne, and 1,600 miles off course. It was probably the worst navigation error in the history of aviation.

The Co-pilot received injuries to his scalp in the forced landing, and died of strain and heat exhaustion a few days later. Fortunately no-one else was killed, and the rest of the crew and passengers were soon rescued. But when investigators eventually arrived on the scene (on camels) they found the entire aircraft gone, stolen piecemeal by Bedouins.

One of the unjustly forgotten pioneers of aviation is Miss Harriet Quimby. Small, pretty, and catlike, she was the first woman to gain a US flying license, and the first woman to fly across the English Channel.

On 1 July 1912, at Squantum Field, near Boston, Massachussetts, as part of a meet being held by the Atlantic Flying Club, she set off to fly a twenty-mile return trip to Boston Light, a course recently flown in a display by the famous British aviator Claude Grahame-White. She was flying a pure white Blériot monoplane, and in it with her, as a passenger, was William A.P. Willard, who was managing the meet.

Some five thousand spectators watched as they set off. They flew to Boston Light, reaching a height of around 5,000 feet, turned, and set off back. About twenty minutes after they had taken off, shortly after 6pm, the spectators at Squantum Field saw them reappear. Miss Quimby was gliding down to land, with her motor switched off.

There was a slight but gusty breeze, and the plane was seen to be wobbling slightly. Suddenly, while still at a height of about 500 feet, it tipped almost vertical and Miss Quimby and Mr Willard, both unbelted, were tipped out. They turned over and over as they fell towards the waters of Dorchester Bay. Where they landed the water was only five feet deep, and both bodies buried themselves deep in the mud of the bottom.

Ironically, the aircraft, freed of its passengers, glided off gracefully into the wind and landed on the water on an even keel. Although it then drove its nose into the mud and turned on its back, it was almost undamaged.

It was the summer of 1967, and pilot Roberts Karns had been hired to drop parachutists over Ohio, aiming for them to land at Ortner Airport, near Cleveland. His plane was a North American B-25, and on his first trip he dropped two of them, who landed safely. Then he took up a further eighteen.

The day was windy, with gusts of 58 mph buffeting his plane. Also it was cloudy, and he dropped the eighteen from 20,000 feet, when he was above a cloud-bank lying at 4,500 to 6,000 feet. This was illegal, except in emergency. He had also, in estimating his position, wrongly assumed that the stiff wind had veered from south-westerly to northerly. Thus he was not where he thought he was. This situation was made worse by the Cleveland Air Traffic Control, who had mistaken for his plane on their radar a little Cessna 180, which was up there to photograph the event. The parachutists, emerging down through the cloud, opened their parachutes at about 3,000 feet, and found they were heading into Lake Erie. The lake was about forty feet deep in this area, and sixteen of them drowned, only two being near enough the shore to be rescued.

By the terms of the Versailles Treaty, signed at the end of the Great War, Germany was forbidden to use powered aircraft. This led to an enormous interest there in the art of gliding, and the centre of world gliding between the wars came to be the huge rounded slopes of the Wasserkuppe, one of the Rhön mountains.

By 1938 much investigation had been going on into towering thunderclouds, and whether there was a safe way to harness the lift that their updraughts undoubtedly provided. A meeting to investigate such clouds was arranged that August (the best time of year to investigate thunderstorms) at Wasserkuppe.

A few days into the meeting, the weather came just right. The air was hot and sultry, and during the afternoon pink thunderheads began to form. As the storm approached, and the sky darkened, the wind dropped. One by one, gliders were launched, and flew to contact the storm. Some brave pilots disappeared up into the dark cloud.

The storm proved unexpectedly fierce. Rain and hail began to pelt, and pilots who had failed to reach the cloud hastened to land. Then the darkness passed overhead, and the sky became grey, with remnants of freezing rain. But no gliders that had entered the cloud were seen to return. What had happened?

Some were indeed safe. Encountering updraughts of over 100 feet per second, Captain Drechsel, of the newly-formed Luftwaffe, had created a new height record, reaching 6,687 metres, and several others had exceeded 5,500 metres, all landing safely in distant fields. But thunderclouds have downdraughts that are just as strong as their updraughts, and both can be close together. In the turbulence between these, a number of gliders had simply broken into pieces.

Amazingly, all the pilots of these had managed to parachute out of their plunging, disintegrating machines. All landed safely but three, whose names were Lemm, Schultz and Blech.

Unknown to each other, but possibly quite close together, they had leapt from their gliders into freezing hail and the darkness of the cloud, and instead of gently falling to earth had found themselves swept upwards by the wind. Rising towards the top of the cloud, they encountered downdraughts, and were swept downwards until an updraught seized them again, and again up they went, unable to drop to the ground.

Up and down like yo-yos they went, in the freezing cold, probably as low as minus 30 degrees celsius. Gradually they were covered with ice, like giant hailstones, and when the cloud did at long last release them, they were dead. (One had also been struck by lightning. Such clouds have lightning too.)

In 1972, at the Executive Airport in Sacramento, California, there was an F-86 Supersabre jet. It was some twenty years old, and had been decommissioned. In fact it was now intended for shipping to Canada to be used as a monument, and in preparation for this it had been stripped down to its essentials. Among other things, a vital centre section of its structure had been removed – a section that supported the wings. Pilot Richard Bingham, not knowing all this, decided to try flying it.

As he raced down the runway, he felt the plane vibrating strangely, but he did not abort because (he later said) he felt confident it would fly. Only it didn't. It skidded on takeoff and ploughed into an ice-cream parlour where around a hundred people were having a birthday party. He killed twenty-two of them.

A Flight-Lieutenant in the RAF was proud to be a member of the elite Red Arrows aerobatic team. One day in 1969 he was flying with them in a Folland Gnat when he heard over his radio the order, 'You are on fire! Eject!' Like any good member of the armed forces, he obeyed the order instantly. He baled out and, as he descended, saw his £400,000 plane hit the ground and disintegrate. But the message hadn't been for him.

10

All at Sea

The sea voyage, the most romantic of all journeys, can be so treacherous that the most indolent researcher could fill an almanac with a hundred shipwrecks for every day of the year (Dr Johnson's comment was that being on a ship was akin to being in jail with the additional chance of being drowned). But sometimes, from some quirk of unkind fate, or moment of inattention, or piece of dumb stupidity, there arises a sea-related misfortune that holds the sort of poetic strangeness that can haunt the dreams . . .

On 21 October 1836, a circus and menagerie, touring Canada, boarded the newly-built paddle-steamer *Royal Tar* at Saint John, in New Brunswick, to sail to Portland, Maine. Among the side-shows were 'Dexter's Locomotive Museum', and 'Burgess's Collection of Serpents and Birds'. The circus, as well as its performers and crew and brass band, had horses, two lions, two camels, a Royal Bengal tiger, a gnu, two pelicans, and Mogul the elephant.

Rising winds and heavy seas delayed her, forcing her to seek shelter, and 25 October found her anchored in the lee of Fox Island, five miles from land. There a succession of blunders caused one of the boilers to run dry. It grew red-hot, and within minutes the ship was ablaze. Realising she was lost, the Captain ordered his men to slip anchor, hoist a distress signal, and lower the lifeboats.

In order to accommodate all his passengers and their animals and gear, several lifeboats had been left behind, so there were not enough to go round. But circus folk are resourceful, and by tearing up deck-boards a number of them managed to build a substantial raft. This they manhandled over the side into the heavy sea. They got themselves onto it, and were about to push off, when Mogul the elephant appeared at the railing above them. He paused for only a moment before jumping on them, killing many and smashing the raft to bits. In a storm at sea, with your ship ablaze and sinking, it is regarded as bad luck to be jumped on by an elephant.

Sir George Tryon, KCB, had for years been a successful officer in the Royal Navy. In his early days he had served in the Crimea, and by 1882 he had risen to be Secretary of the Admiralty. In 1884 he was promoted to the rank of Rear-Admiral, and in 1889 to Vice-Admiral.

By 1893 he was commanding the navy's Mediterranean Station, and on 22 June was off Tripoli, directing manoeuvres. His flagship, the *Victoria*, was leading one line of six battleships, and in a parallel line, twelve hundred yards to port, were five others, led by the *Camperdown*.

On his order, the eleven ships sailed past their anchorage. Then he gave the order for both lines of ships, staying in column, to turn inwards and return towards it. The smallest turning-circle of both leading ships was officially stated to be six hundred yards, but in practice was something nearer eight hundred. As a result, some brave officers, knowing there would not be enough room, questioned his order, but in the full confidence of command he sternly repeated it, and the manoeuvre began. In under four minutes the *Victoria* and the *Camperdown* collided, the ram on the prow of the *Camperdown* holing and sinking the *Victoria*, which overturned, its racing screws killing many in the water. There were 357 men lost, including Admiral Tryon himself.

Bill Quinlan who was 48, and his nephew, David Lucas, aged 18, were sailing a forty-foot trimaran across the Pacific in 1978. San Diego, in California, to the Galapagos Islands: En route they were hit by a hurricane. The trimaran overturned, but the two of them managed to free a life-raft and get onto it.

They drifted on the raft for five days, seeing no-one. Then Bill told his nephew there was not enough food aboard for the two of them. Nobly he wished his nephew good luck, dived into the sea, and swam away, never to be seen again. David was rescued next day by a Mexican fishing-boat, with a considerable store of his provisions still untouched.

The *Mignonette* was a little 19-ton yawl, and in 1884 Captain Thomas Dudley had the unenviable task of sailing her halfway round the world, from Southampton to Australia, to deliver her to the man who had bought her.

He had a crew of three – Edward Stephens (mate), Edmund Brooks (third hand) and Richard Parker (boy).

He had serious doubts about the *Mignonette* making the voyage, and these were justified when, on 5 July, she was swamped in a gale by a huge wave, and sank within five minutes. During those five minutes, however, the crew did manage to launch and get into a 14-foot open dinghy, taking with them a compass, a sextant, a chronometer, and two tins of turnips. They would have had fresh water as well, but the boy Parker, thinking it would float, had thrown the water barrel into the sea. It didn't.

They were now in mid-Atlantic, more or less level with the southern end of Africa, and some three hundred miles off the east-Atlantic trade routes. With so little food, and nothing to drink, they would soon have starved, but fortunately they caught a turtle.

Even so, after sixteen days they were in a desperate situation. Captain Dudley had organised the rigging of a sail, and he reckoned that in another week they would have travelled a thousand miles east and reached the South American trade routes. But attempts to catch fish had failed and they desperately needed food.

After a day's deliberation, he reluctantly decided that one of them must die in order to keep the other three alive. To draw lots, he felt, would be a hypocrisy, as the crew could not afford to lose him. That being said, he knew it was his responsibility to decide which of the others it should be. It was a small relief that this was quite easy. The boy Parker alone had no mother, wife, or children. Furthermore, he had disobeyed orders the previous day and drunk sea-water, and as a result had now fallen into coma and delirium. On 24 July Dudley killed him by cutting his throat.

Five days later the others were picked up by a German barque, the *Montezuma*. Back in England, all three were charged with murder. Brooks, the third hand, was soon discharged, and gave evidence. The other two were convicted and sentenced to death, but, given the circumstances, this was commuted to six months without hard labour.

By one of the oddest coincidences, there is a short novel by Edgar Allen Poe, called *The Narrative of A. Gordon Pym*, in which four men, similarly adrift and foodless on an almost-submerged brig, draw lots to see which of their number shall be killed for food. Not only was the losing man's name Richard Parker, but Captain Dudley had a copy of the story in his cabin aboard the *Mignonette*.

On an afternoon in June 1811, a labourer, John Hall, went out at low tide among the rocks at Hume Head, near Cawsand, in Cornwall, to look for crabs. When the tide recedes from the rocks, crabs hide in crevices in them. Hall, searching these crevices, put his hand into one. As luck would have it, it did contain a crab – a large one, which promptly gripped his hand with its pincers. Crabs, once they have hold of something, are programmed not to let go, and this one held on till the tide rose and fell again, when John Hall was found drowned, still gripped.

Henry Hall was a tough old boy. Although 94 years of age, he was one of the three keepers manning the second Eddystone lighthouse (the one designed by John Rudyerd), 14 miles off Plymouth in the English Channel. One midnight, at the beginning of December in 1755, he was alone on the middle watch. Although the night was bitterly cold, with a stiff wind, the sea was not really rough. But the 70-foot-high lighthouse was built only of wood, and from time to time a large wave would strike its side, making it shudder.

Henry climbed up into the lantern-room to inspect the bunch of large tallow candles that provided the light. He checked how many spare candles there were, trimmed a couple of wicks that were smoking, and replaced a couple of candles that were almost burned out. Then he retreated down to the snug of the kitchen.

From time to time he again went up to check the candles. But at 2am, setting off to make one of these inspections, he found his way up barred by clouds of black smoke. The lantern was on fire.

The floor immediately below the lantern-room was the gallery floor, and outside on the encircling gallery was a rain-barrel. Grabbing a leather bucket, he began trying to hurl bucketfuls of rainwater up towards the lantern, at the same time yelling to try and rouse the other two keepers. But they were sleeping several floors below, and what with the wind and the waves it was some time before he could make them hear.

When they did hear, they joined in helping, running

up and down the narrow stairway fetching buckets of seawater. But it was hopeless – the copper chimney of the lantern, corroded by seawater, had allowed a spark to escape into the crust of soot and tallow-grease that had collected inside the leaden cupola that roofed the lantern during nearly fifty years of use.

Trying for hours to throw buckets of water upwards was hard enough, but at length the cupola itself began to melt. Henry Hall was throwing yet another bucketful upwards when the wooden beams supporting the cupola burnt through, and a rain of molten lead came down on him, burning his hair and face and arms. His mouth was open, and a considerable amount passed down his throat into his stomach.

The wooden summit of the lighthouse was now ablaze, and the three keepers, giving up, realised that their best hope was to try and find shelter below till they were rescued. As the wooden structure burned, red-hot clamps and bolts started to shower down all round it, and for this reason they tried for a while to shelter deep inside. But as the fire crept down, floor by floor, their minds turned to a cleft they knew of in the Eddystone rock itself. This was covered by the sea at high tide, so they had to wait, but eventually they judged the tide would be low enough, and ran for it, dodging the hail of burning debris. In it, drenched by waves, they sheltered until ten in the morning, when a fishing-boat arrived and took them off, hauling them aboard one by one through the sea on a rope.

Once ashore at Plymouth, one of the two younger keepers took off, and was never seen again. People said his mind had been unhinged by his experiences. The other was not too badly hurt. But poor old Henry Hall was. He lingered for twelve days, insisting to disbelieving doctors that he had swallowed molten lead, which they believed would be impossible to survive.

After he died, an autopsy was performed, and true enough, a flat oval lump of lead was found in his stomach. It was four inches long, weighed almost half a pound, and is now in the Royal Scottish Museum, Edinburgh.

On a Saturday in December, 1784, in Kingston, Jamaica, the schooner *Highfield* was moored offshore, and some members of its crew came ashore for a night on the town. Returning to the waterside at about 10pm, they found a boat waiting at the wharf to row them out to their ship.

Unfortunately one of their number, a cooper named Richard Page, had had a few, and he declared that he didn't need a boat – he would swim out. His companions tried to dissuade him, and their discussion went on for some time, eventually turning into a physical tussle. Then Page broke free, ran to the edge of the wharf, and leapt into the sea, followed by a large Newfoundland dog that happened to be hanging around.

He struck out for the *Highfield*, and the others swiftly got into the boat and set off after him. But they had hardly gone ten yards when they heard Page cry out. He had been severely bitten by a shark. Rowing to where he was, they managed to get him into the boat, mangled and dying. The shark had to content itself with eating the dog. (Sharks, by the way, become mindlessly over-excited at the faintest scent of blood, so the tip to remember if you're ever attacked by sharks is 'don't bleed'.)

In 1923 seven United States Navy torpedo-boat destroyers were sailing as a flotilla, with one leading the other six. The leader was the *Delphy*, and the others, in order, were the S.P. Lee, the *Young*, the *Nicholas*, the *Woodbury*, the *Chauncey*, and the *Fuller*. The officer in charge was Captain Edward H. Watson, and they were off the coast of California, travelling at a steady speed of twenty knots in a dense fog.

Captain Watson believed they were some eight miles clear of land, and so had plenty of sea room. But he was wrong. They were just off the island of Santa Barbara. Without any warning, the leading ship, the *Delphy*, crashed onto the rocks at Honda Point. The *Young* ran into her propellors, gashing her own side open, and the *Chauncey* ran into the pair of them. The four others then simply ran onto the rocks independently. All became total wrecks.

Luckily, of the 500 officers and men aboard the seven ships, only 22 died. At first, investigators thought that the cause of the faulty navigation might have been exceptional tides caused by the great Tokyo earthquake of a week earlier, but this proved not to be so. It was simply the sort of mistake anybody might make.

The Smalls was an early lighthouse, built on stilts on the Smalls rocks in 1775. It was some twenty-odd miles off the coast of Pembrokeshire, in south-west Wales. Its keepers were on duty in pairs, for a month at a time, and one pair was Thomas Howell and Thomas Griffiths. They had been known for years as close friends, although fiercely argumentative (they could become so vehement, without coming to blows, that they had been known to clear bars).

In 1780, early in their tour of duty, Howell suddenly dropped dead in the lantern room, hitting his head on a stanchion as he fell. This put Griffiths in something of a spot. He was afraid he might be accused of killing him during one of their arguments if he simply buried him in the sea. His only recourse seemed to be to keep him. So he used the wood of a cupboard to construct a makeshift coffin, and put Howell into it.

Then ferocious autumn storms blew up, preventing anyone from reaching the Smalls. Also, Howell's body began to decompose, so Griffiths moved the coffin outside onto the gallery surrounding the lantern-room, lashing it with ropes to the gallery railings. But the storms continued. Waves pounding the gallery broke open the flimsy coffin, and Howell's body tumbled out, lying on the floor of the gallery with one arm hanging through the railings. The crew of a boat, trying to get near, saw this arm moving in the storm, and assumed it was one of the keepers waving in greeting.

No boat was able to reach the lighthouse for two

months. Griffiths kept the light burning every night, but the stress of the responsibility, and the presence of his dead friend for so long, damaged his mind. Once relieved, it was said that people he knew found it hard to recognise him, and he was never the same again. He died in a madhouse twenty years later.

He was never suspected of killing his friend, but the incident caused a change in lighthouse practice. From then on, rock lighthouses were always manned by three keepers.

In 1918 a Russian submarine named *Igor* (or possibly *Ugor*) was on manoeuvres in the Baltic Sea, somewhere off Rewal, in Poland. It was on the surface, and the Captain, through his first Officer, gave the order to make a practice dive. This would of course mean closing all the hatches.

Unfortunately these were the early days of the Soviet Union. The Revolution had taken place less than six months before, and all good Russians were for the time being in a state of euphoria, believing that from now on no aristocracy (or anyone else) could give them orders. Everyone was now everyone else's equal. And as this order happened to be given during one of the crew's rest periods, the man whose job it was to close the after hatch decided it was unconstitutional. He simply sat there and watched the Baltic flow in.

The submarine sank, and all aboard were lost, except,

as it happened, the Captain and first Officer. They were sent to Siberia for giving an illegal and harsh order. The crew were, after all, taking their rest.

11

On the Road

There used to be a romance to the road – in Britain in the Twenties and Thirties motoring was a pleasant and fairly civilised activity; in America in the Fifties 'the road' was a poetic idea, a journey leading to who-knows-what new life, new scenes, new people, new experiences. But somehow the majesty and mystery of the open road doesn't seem to last. Roads get congested, or neglected (remember how barely-existent they were for years after the train replaced the stage-coach). In America even the famous Route 66 has now, in Bill Bryson's words, become 'a series of back highways and anonymous frontage roads'. All the same, while they are with us, they do invite misfortune.

In Wupperthal in 1986, a West German woman aged 56 returned from shopping to her car. In it she had left her cat, and after apologising to it for being so long, she began to drive home. The cat bit her.

As a result, she lost control and collided with a parked car. Then she hit and demolished a sausage-vendor's stand. This, collapsing, dragged a fish-frying stand down with it, burning an assistant with boiling fat. Which caused a passer-by to faint.

The car was a write-off, and she and the cat had to be driven home by the police. She later received a demand for DM 100,000 damages (then the equivalent to around £26,000).

Chris Lane, aged 31, was a council worker. In 1979, in Rowley Regis, on the outskirts of Birmingham, he was driving a road roller when suddenly its brakes failed. Careering down a hill, he managed to swing it off the road onto an empty pathway. Empty, that is, apart from tools and materials belonging to men doing resurfacing. His roller demolished a wheelbarrow and headed towards an open manhole. It was at this moment that 19-year-old Chris Priest, working down the manhole, stuck his head out to find out what all the rumbling was. It was the last thing he learned.

In 1987, on a highway near the Andalusian town of Huelva, in Spain, two cars collided violently. The driver of one, who was alone, was a hairdresser's assistant from Seville. Her name was Maria del Amor Maceda. The driver of the other, Santiago Lopez, had with him his fiancée, Maria Nieves Trijueque, who was a computer programming student. All three were removed from the wreckage and taken to hospital.

Santiago was not too badly injured. He remained unconscious for a week, but shortly after he regained consciousness, he was discharged. The two girls fared far worse. His fiancée, Maria Nieves, died shortly after reaching the hospital. It turned out that she was not carrying identity papers, and a careless official wrote the name of the other girl, Maria del Amor, on the death certificate. The grieving family of Maria del Amor buried her, and the real Maria del Amor, lying injured in hospital, was naturally accepted as the real Maria Nieves.

Both girls were 'dark blondes' with blue eyes, both had been of similar build, and the surviving Maria had facial injuries – her face was swollen and connected to tubes. After a period in intensive care, regularly visited by the other Maria's family, she was taken to their home and lovingly tended. Repeatedly she tried to explain to these unknown parents, brothers and sisters that she was not who they thought, but their reaction was only to wonder sadly if she would ever recover her mind.

Admittedly there were some things that slightly worried them. Why did she have braces on her teeth? Why had her skin darkened a little? Why were her eyebrows plucked? How come her blue eyes no longer had that faint greenish tint they had all been so fond of? Doctors had ready answers. Her teeth must have been damaged in the crash. Medical treatment can affect skin colour. A nurse had plucked her eyebrows. Eye colour can change.

And why did she keep muttering that she was Maria del Amor? Because in her shock and confusion she must be repeating what the other girl had moaned in the ambulance.

To make matters worse for Maria, Santiago, once recovered and discharged, totally accepted her as his fiancée. Did not the clothes in her bedroom wardrobe, Maria Nieves' clothes, fit her perfectly?

Her nightmare ordeal only came to an end when a member of her real family, becoming suspicious, managed to disguise herself as a visiting nurse, get into the bedroom she was in, and take a surreptitious photo of her. It was convincing enough for the authorities to arrange for her fingerprints to be taken, which proved she was who she was. She had been fighting to assert her own identity, in a nightmare of pain and confusion, for eight weeks.

Biagio di Crescenzio lived in Rome. One spring day in 1974 he was driving near the small town of Fondi, about sixty miles south-east of there, when his car skidded off the road and hit a tree.

He was quite badly injured, and a passing motorist, seeing the wreck, got him out of it and drove him to the hospital in Fondi. There he hovered between life and death, and the hospital authorities, realising he needed more specialist treatment than they could provide, decided to send him to Rome in an ambulance. The ambulance had travelled only a few miles when it was seriously hit by an oncoming car.

Another passing motorist, seeing this second wreck, got di Crescenzio out of the back and into his car, and took him to another hospital in Latina (about forty miles south-east of Rome). His condition continued to worsen, and the Latina doctors again decided he should be sent to Rome in an ambulance.

This time the ambulance got ten miles before it skidded into another car. This time di Crescenzio was killed.

In 1980 in the African kingdom of Burundi, a lorry had two drivers. One of them, during a stop, decided that, as it was his companion's turn to drive, he would ride in the back and have a snooze. Climbing aboard, and observing that there seemed to be a chance of rain, he crawled into an empty coffin they were carrying, and closed the lid.

He had a pleasant snooze, and waking, raised the lid. But as luck would have it, while he was asleep his co-driver had picked up five hitch-hikers, who were also riding in the back. Terrified at seeing a man emerge from a coffin, they leapt off. The truck was travelling at high speed, and all died.

In 1978 the Australian Safety Committee organised a group of nurses to push a hospital bed 2,000 miles from Hobart to Perth. This was, of course, to publicise a charity, and as the nurses explained, 'We want to prevent careless accidents.'

Along the route, one of them fell under the advancing bed, and a castor broke her neck.

Mike Stewart was president of the Auto Convoy Company of Dallas, Texas. Dallas had many low bridges, and Mike became convinced that some of them were a traffic hazard. In 1983 he decided to put the problem before the civic authorities, and as part of his presentation decided to make a movie showing the most dangerous spots. So he hired a camera crew, loaded them and their equipment into the back of one of his trucks, got into it with them, and set off round the city. As the truck passed under one of the low bridges in question he became decapitated.

12

Off the Rails

The train is of course the most poetic of all forms of transport – the Blue Train, the Twentieth Century Limited, the Orient Express, the Trans-Siberia Railway. No wonder it has inspired so many musical compositions – 'Chattanooga Choo Choo', 'Pacific 231', 'Coronation Scot', 'Daybreak Express' – and paintings as varied as The Railway Station *and* Rain, Steam and Speed. *And trains are safe – or at least mostly; even among railway songs there are those like 'Casey Jones', 'The Ballad of John Axon' and 'The Wreck of the Old 97' that involve crashes. And when they do crash the wreckage is immense. The railway writer L.T.C. Rolt once pointed out that no train-wreck created for a film ever came anywhere near the wholesale destruction of a real rail disaster. So much power is concealed within the elegant shell of a steam locomotive that even a simple misfortune can be elegantly dramatic.*

The year was 1850 and an engine was standing in the station yard at Wolverton (at that time part of the London & Birmingham Railway). It had been standing for some time, with its fire blazing merrily, so, naturally, it had built up a considerable head of steam. So much, in fact, that the safety valve, installed to prevent pressure building up to a dangerous level, had opened, and steam was noisily escaping. It was making such a noise, and for so long, that a labourer working nearby decided to do something about it. Which he did by the simple expedient of climbing up onto the engine and screwing the valve down shut. This stopped the steam blowing off, and he returned to his work satisfied. A few minutes later the whole engine dramatically exploded. With poetic justice, a flying fragment sliced off one of his ears.

Events on the Great Northern Railway of Ireland, on the morning of Wednesday, 12th June 1889, were such a confusion of casual bad practice that an accident was almost bound to happen.

That day there was to be a special excursion train taking schoolchildren on a trip from Armagh to the coastal town of Warrenpoint, a little over twenty miles away. Events began early in the morning when engine-driver Thomas McGrath collected at Dundalk an engine and thirteen empty coaches. For a start, he had never in his life driven over the line from Armagh to Warrenpoint. Furthermore, bookings for the excursion had been heavy, so en route to Armagh, when he stopped at Portisdown, two additional empty coaches were added to his train.

This worried McGrath, as the line out of Armagh began with a stiff three-mile gradient, and he was not sure that the engine he had chosen would be able to haul fifteen fully laden coaches up it. So at Armagh, while the children and their attendant adults climbed aboard, he went to the stationmaster's office and protested. He complained that he had been told to expect no more than thirteen coaches, and, if he'd known, he would have brought a more powerful engine.

The stationmaster, John Foster, told him severely that it was not a driver's job to grumble about having to take an excursion train. Words were exchanged, and eventually McGrath left the office in a temper and returned to his engine.

Foster also left his office and, on the platform, encountered the man who was in charge of organising the excursion. His name was James Elliot, he was chief clerk to the Superintendent of the line, and it had been arranged that he would travel with McGrath on the footplate of his engine. Foster told him of McGrath's foolish objections, and Elliot suggested a plan of action. A regular train was to be next along the line after them, and as it was standing by, its engine might be used to assist the excursion up the three-mile gradient from the rear, after which it could return to Armagh for its own train.

This unorthodox suggestion might have worked, but objections were raised that the engine wouldn't have time, if it was to keep to its own schedule. Someone else suggested that maybe some of the excursion passengers could be transferred to the regular train, which was expected to be lightly loaded.

Elliot, undecided about all this, went to join McGrath on his engine to ask what he thought. But McGrath's temper had now turned to an angry pride in his engine and his ability, and he insisted that of course they could do it. Elliot thus went and cancelled all other arrangements, then joined McGrath on the footplate. McGrath, with a full head of steam, charged towards the foot of the incline, the coaches behind him crammed with 340 adults and 600 children, and with their doors locked, which was standard practice for any excursion involving children. Even the guard's van at the rear had passengers travelling in it. There were fifteen of them, and some began horsing around with the mechanical hand-brake there, turning its wheel to try and slow the train for a joke.

In spite of this, and the load, the engine did fairly well for the first couple of miles up the climb. But near the top, within sight of the summit, the steam-pressure had dropped so much it came to a standstill. McGrath and Elliot discussed the situation, and Elliot decided the thing to do would be to split the train in two, so that the engine could haul the first five coaches over the summit to the next station, and then return for the rest.

The problem with this bright idea was that dividing the train would mean uncoupling the air-line operating the brakes on all the coaches. On later trains, uncoupling the air-line caused all the brakes to lock on, but on trains of this time it released them. So to get round this problem Elliot proposed to screw down the brake in the rear guard's van (which was the train's only other brake). Having done this, he made extra sure by putting a few stones under the wheels of the topmost coach.

All this was done, and the guard of the front part of the train, William Moorhead, had just undone the coupling between the two halves of the train when McGrath, thinking to help him uncouple by giving him a bit of slack, without warning set back his engine. It bumped the coaches back against each other, knocking away the chocking stones. And the hand-brake did not hold, possibly because of holidaymakers playing with it on the way up the gradient.

Gradually the runaway coaches picked up speed. Moorhead, racing alongside, tried to drop the coupling back over its hook. Twice he nearly succeeded, but tripped and fell. He tried throwing more stones under the wheels, but they were simply knocked away. The guard at the rear managed to jump back into his van and screw the hand-brake down harder, but it did not help.

As the coaches gathered more speed, the rear guard and the fifteen passengers with him managed to jump to safety, but all the rest were locked in. They were in a state of panic as their coaches, by now wildly rocking, tore down the incline. Halfway down they met the regular train coming up.

Three of the packed coaches were completely demolished, their wreckage strewn down the embankments either side of the line. It was Ireland's worst railway accident. Eighty people, mostly children, died.

Many electric trains have what is called a 'dead man's handle', a lever which the driver must hold down or the train will stop. This is a precaution against the drivers fainting or falling ill. In 1926 a local train running in the Newcastle-upon-Tyne area had such a handle, but the driver, William Skinner, finding it a nuisance, tied it down with two handkerchiefs. With the train still merrily proceeding on its way, he then wandered back into the luggage compartment behind his cab, and for some reason stuck his head out of the window to try and peer into the passenger saloon behind it. He was decapitated by a stanchion supporting an iron bridge. Fortunately no-one else was hurt, although the train did career on, driver-less, for another mile. There it entered Manors station and was brought to rest by crashing into a stationary goods train.

The worst head-on collision in the history of the British railway system occurred on a dark night in 1874, as the result of a very human series of blunders. At Thorpe station, in Norwich, the express from Liverpool Street to Yarmouth was late, and the question arose whether to call up the mail train from neighbouring Brundall, in the other direction, before it arrived. The line between the two stations had only a single track.

The night inspector, whose name was Cooper, mistak-enly believed that the stationmaster had agreed to let the mail be run first. So he went to the station's telegraph office and asked Robson, the young clerk there, to order it up from Brundall. The procedure laid down was for Robson to write the order on a pad, and for Cooper to sign it before it was transmitted. But before young Robson had finished writing it, Cooper hurried away.

One minute later, the express pulled in, and the day inspector, Parker, asked Cooper if he had ordered the mail up. Cooper, not having signed the order, replied that he had not, and Parker thereupon ordered the express to set off on its way to Brundall.

Cooper, wanting to tell young Robson that the mail was not to be ordered up just yet, hurried to the telegraph office. There he found Robson anxiously asking someone if it was true that the express had just left. It turned out that in a misguided attempt to be helpful he had telegraphed the order to send the mail. 'You told me to,' he said to Cooper, then hurried to his instruments and sent the message to Brundall, 'Stop mail'. Back came the deadly reply, 'Mail left'.

It was an appalling situation. The night was dark and rainy, with visibility down to 300 yards, and two trains were heading for each other on a single track, with no possible means of warning or recalling them. There was nothing to do but wait.

After some minutes the waiting station staff heard a sound like 'a great roar of thunder'. No-one could tell the exact details of the collision, for both engine-crews perished. In all, twenty-five lives were lost and seventy-three were injured.

A final irony is that a double line was already laid between the two stations, waiting only for the Board of Trade to inspect it before it could be used.

An unusual railway disaster, and one of the worst, occurred in Italy on the night of 2 March 1944, during the Second World War. By this time Mussolini's Fascist Party had fallen, and Italy, under its new government, had switched sides, joining the Allies. But there was still much fighting on Italian soil, and everywhere wartime conditions prevailed.

For a start, there was a flourishing black market, and one train in particular, which ran every Thursday night between the city of Naples and the country region of Lucania, was known as 'the black market special'. Black-marketeers would travel through the night to Lucania, stuff their empty suitcases with meats, grain, vegetables, oils, tobacco and sweets, and next day bring them back to Naples. Technically this was illegal, but food was so scarce in the city that officials turned a blind eye.

As it happened, the train in question was hardly a passenger train at all. It was mostly a big long goods train, which on this night was made up of 42 empty boxcars, a mere four coaches, and a guard's van, all hauled by two engines. When it left the town of Balvano, at fifty minutes after midnight on a freezing morning, there were no fewer than 521 passengers aboard, most of them having clambered illegally into the empty boxcars as the train slowly picked up speed out of Naples station. Not quite all were black-marketeers. A few were ordinary farmers or businessmen, seizing the only way available up over the mountains (apart from walking), and there was a party of medical students who, with their professor, were returning from a hospital field trip. There were also the six railway workers – two crew on each engine, plus a conductor and a brakeman.

The mountains were the forbidding Apennines, and from Balvano the rise was steep. The rails were icy, and the wartime coal the engines had for fuel was poor. And with all the extra unofficial passengers, the weight of the train was slightly more than the two engines hauling it were designed to pull.

The next station, Bella-Muro, was 3 or 4 miles away, and in that distance were several tunnels. The third and longest of these, the Galleria delle Armi, burrowed through the forested mountains for two miles.

The engines, stoked up to haul the heavy load, had been smoking furiously from the time they left Balvano. Nonetheless, as the train entered the steeply-climbing Galleria delle Armi, it slowed and stopped. All of it was inside the tunnel except the guard's van, at the very rear.

It is believed that the driver of the leading engine suggested building up steam for a moment, then forging on, while the driver of the second engine suggested reversing back down out of the tunnel. But no-one will ever know for sure, because within moments both crews had passed out and died, poisoned by the vast amounts of carbon monoxide in the smoke from the poorly-burning coal. The train stood, still pouring out smoke.

In the guard's van there was a pot-bellied stove, and brakeman Michele Palo was huddled over it for warmth in the bitter night. After the train stopped, he did nothing for a while. He had heard no warning whistle from the engines, and assumed the train had stopped at a signal. Eventually, reluctantly, he pulled on his gloves and stepped out into the sleet.

He had gone no further than a hundred feet into the pitch-black tunnel when the meaning of the total silence struck him. Appalled, he turned and began to run the two miles back to Balvano, stumbling and slipping over the sleepers. He gashed his leg and sprained his wrist and got splinters in his fingers, but at 2.50 am he arrived there, shouting, 'Up there! Up the track! They're all dead!'

The assistant stationmaster organised an engine, and when it eventually arrived at the stalled train he found it was all too true. Five passengers did survive, but 516 had peacefully died, plus the two engine crews and the conductor.

Of the five who survived, three were black-marketeers, who made haste to totally disappear. One of the others received permanent brain damage from the fumes, and was never able to give any useful evidence. The fifth, an olive oil salesman called Domenico Miele, owed his survival to having wrapped a scarf around his face against the cold. This had saved him from anything worse than passing out.

Relatives of the dead did try to sue for damages, but seven years later, in 1951, their suits were ruled out of order, on the grounds that the railways at the time were officially being run by the Allied Military Government, who could not be held responsible for a 'wartime accident'.

13

The Fog of War

War is hell. So much so that the stress, fatigue and appre-hension it brings with it soon lead to that state of confusion known to military tacticians as 'the fog of war'. This usually sets in with the first shot fired, after which nobody on either side is quite sure what is happening. Orders are misinter-preted, and intelligence reports are liable to be inaccurate, conflicting, or misunderstood. To list the unfortunate cock-ups of war – soldiers firing on their allies, troops failing to rendezvous, equipment failing – would fill a library. But some are even more extraordinary than others.

During the Second World War, a British bomber made a raid on Germany. It was of course at night, and there was also a heavy fog, so visibility was almost nil. Which made it doubly unfortunate that the pilot, heading for home, accidentally set off on exactly the opposite compass bearing to the one he should have taken. It took him a while to realise what he'd done, but when he did he at once turned round and set off in the right direction. However, he knew that now he would most likely run out of fuel before reaching Britain. The best he could hope for would be to land somewhere in Holland, then occupied by the Germans.

His fuel did eventually run out, but he managed to make a reasonably good landing in a large field. He and his crew scrambled out. There was a standing order that any air-crew forced to land in occupied territory were to set fire to their plane, to prevent it falling into enemy hands. This they did and, once they were sure that the fire had taken a good hold, pilot and crew tramped off across the field. Reaching a hedge, they looked over, and by the light of their burning plane beheld a pub called the Rose and Crown. They were already safely back in England.

In 1936, Dr Herman Goertz, a veteran of the Great War, was convicted of spying, not very effectively, on British airfields, and sentenced to four years in Maidstone gaol. Among his fellow-prisoners were several members of the Irish Republican Army, and he learned that the IRA, or some branches of it, had a plan to help Germany invade and unify Ireland.

This plan, codenamed Kathleen, had been submitted to Military Intelligence in Hamburg, who had decided, somewhat half-heartedly, to go along with it. Thus, when Dr Goertz was released in 1939, he made his way home to Germany and contacted Military Intelligence, who again enrolled him as a spy and inducted him into the Luftwaffe reserve with the rank of Lieutenant.

The Second World War began, and Eire, to preserve its neutrality, agreed to imprison for the duration of the war any member of either warring working side that entered that country. So when Dr Goertz was dropped by parachute into County Meath, on the night of 5/6 May 1940, he was facing imprisonment if caught. And for once the legendary thoroughness of Nazi Germany failed. He was dropped in the wrong place, he was wearing German uniform, and he was carrying military identity papers (although as a gesture to secrecy these were in a false name). And he himself did not help matters by failing to recover a second parachute, dropping him a container-full of equipment, including a wireless set.

He then set out on foot to a rendezvous he was supposed to make in County Wicklow, some seventy miles away. To get there he had to swim the substantial river Boyne, which he did, as he recalled, 'with great difficulty', losing his invisible ink in the process. Exhausted by hunger and strain, he soon discarded his uniform jacket, and as he said, 'I was now in high boots, breeches and jumper, with a little black beret on my head. . . . I kept my military cap as a vessel for drinks and my war medals for sentimental reasons. . . . I had no Irish money and did not realise that I could use English money quite freely.'

He did make his rendezvous, but soon found himself totally out of his depth in the cross-currents of Irish Nationalist politics, and achieved nothing before he was arrested by the Irish police in November 1941.

The Battle of New Orleans, between England and America, took place in January 1815. The British army, old-fashioned in its strategy, marched in parade-ground formation to confront a line of entrenched backwoodsmen. After only twenty minutes of combat, their Commander, General Pakenham, was killed, and they fled. Two thousand British were killed or wounded. The Americans lost only twenty-one. And what made things worse was that a peace treaty between the nations had been signed in Belgium, in Ghent, two weeks before. Communications in those days were so slow that neither side knew it.

During the Second World War, the American submarine *Tang* was operating in the Pacific. She had a fine success record, having sunk 24 Japanese ships in eight months, but on the night of 24 October 1944, in the Formosa Straits, things suddenly went wrong. She now had only a few torpedoes left, so, when a Japanese convoy was sighted, her captain, Commander Richard H. O'Kane, made sure each one counted.

For a while he was successful, and was pleased with the way things were going. So he was disappointed when his Executive Officer told him that *Tang* was down to her last torpedo. He decided to use it carefully.

He lined *Tang* up on a Japanese escort vessel he had already hit and crippled, and gave the order to fire. But this last torpedo was faulty. Instead of heading straight, it began to wander off to port. In fact it wandered so far that, having missed the escort vessel, it circled round and came heading straight for *Tang* herself.

Commander O'Kane tried to take evasive action, but failed. The torpedo struck *Tang* in the after torpedo room and exploded. He had only time to order the hatch below the conning-tower to be closed before she sank under him, and he found himself treading water in the sea, along with eight other men who had been with him on the bridge. A few moments later a tenth man, Lieutenant Savadkin, who had been in the conning-tower, bobbed up to join them.

Meanwhile *Tang*, with her three stern compartments flooded, sank in 180 feet of water, with 86 men still inside. At which point the Japanese warships escorting the convoy began to harass her with depth charges. They did this deafeningly for four hours, then quit, after which the men still inside her made efforts to get out through the escape hatch.

Out of the four groups who tried escaping, only thirteen men survived the attempt, and of these only five survived the night. These, like Commander O'Kane and the nine with him, were captured and interned by the Japanese. And of these fifteen, only nine survived the war. Commander O'Kane was one, and President Truman awarded him the Congressional Medal of Honor – as an honour to him and as a salute to the men whose submarine sank itself.

Late on the afternoon of 12th March 1918, the crew of a French airship patrolling the North Atlantic spotted a submarine cruising along on the surface. Cunningly, they crept up on it by keeping the sun behind them, so as to be hidden in its glare. They were spotted, however, and the submarine fired rockets at them, but still they succeeded in dropping four 52-kilo bombs. These exploded close to the sub and sank it, with the loss of all aboard. This was the only time ever in the history of warfare that an airship sank a submarine.

It was unfortunate that the submarine was in fact British, and thus fighting on the same side. (The 'rockets' had been signal flares, intended to identify the sub to its allies.)

During the Second World War, the RAF was to demonstrate to the top level of British military leaders the efficiency of its Hurricane fighters in making low-level attacks on enemy troops and transport. Among those expected to attend were Lord Mountbatten, Chief of Combined Operations; Lord Portal, Chief of Air Staff; and Winston Churchill himself.

The demonstration was to take place on Ministry of Defence land at Imber Down, near Warminster, in Wiltshire, on 14 April 1942, and to make sure all went well a dress rehearsal was held the day before. The targets were set out in three parallel lines – one of lorries, one of wooden dummies representing marching soldiers, and one of tanks.

Senior officers – Generals and Brigadiers – watched as Hurricane after Hurricane swept in, each with its twelve Browning .303 machine-guns blazing, each gun firing at 1,200 rounds a minute. The tanks and lorries, filled with petrol to add to the effect, exploded in flame, and the dummy soldiers shattered into splinters. It was enormously impressive.

There was a slight lull, and then another Hurricane came screaming in, piloted by a young Canadian sergeant who had been brought in as a last-minute replacement. Mistaking the line of watching officers for dummies, he raked them with fire, killing 27 and seriously wounding 68.

The actual demonstration, next day, went without a hitch.

It was the autumn of 1939, the Second World War was in its early weeks, and the blackout was still a new thing. Not only had all windows to be curtained so that not a chink of light showed, but the headlights of motor vehicles were reduced to a dim glow. Near Sherborne, in Dorset, four soldiers left an inn late at night and, while walking home along a quiet road, were moved to sit down in the middle of it and sing a hymn. All four were killed by a bus.

14

For the Cause

Ah, the cause! As recently as 1904 so amiable a writer as G.K. Chesterton was writing that if a cause is worthwhile it is worth dying for, or killing for. 'Sanctified by the sword' I think was one of his phrases (after the Great War he no longer uttered such youthful romantic notions). He should have considered that a hundred years earlier Talleyrand had advised, 'Surtout, Messieurs, point de zèle.' And Talleyrand was right. Zeal, or enthusiasm (in its older sense of being consumed by a cause) is deadly. Among zealots, dying for your religion at least makes some kind of sense. They believe that this life is a mere anteroom to Life Everlasting, and that after a short sharp shock they'll wake up in eternal comfort, surrounded by singing zebras or marshmallow maidens or whatever. But there are many (too many) who commit major violence for even an earthly cause.

Laurent Tailhade, living in Paris in the late nineteenth century, was a dandy, a poet, and a leading anarchist writer. There was quite a lot of anarchism around at the time. Some people were inclined to blame this on Wagner's music, which was felt to be 'chaotic', and thus to create, in those who loved it, a love of chaos. Tailhade, who may or may not have liked Wagner, tended to write in a rather florid style, viciously attacking all religious belief and all accepted moral codes.

In December 1893 another anarchist, Auguste Vaillant, threw a sizeable bomb from the upper gallery of the French Chamber of Deputies. He intended it to explode on the floor of the chamber, but his aim was poor and it hit a balustrade, thus detonating in mid-air. Even so, about eighty were wounded, although none fatally. Tailhade, then nearing forty, commented (rather arrogantly), '*Qu'importe la disparition de vagues humanites si le geste est beau!*' This remark brought him wide public notoriety as '*l'Homme au beau geste*'.

Not long afterwards, on 1 April 1894, he was dining in the fashionable Restaurant Foyot (with a certain Mlle Violette), when an anarchist bomb exploded there as well. Tailhade was the only person seriously injured. This new '*beau geste*' wounded him seriously and put out his right eye. Fashionable Paris was considerably amused.

In the same year as Tailhade's misfortune, police agents from various European countries, feeling that the British government was doing nothing to round up anarchists in Britain, infiltrated the flourishing British anarchist movement and talked one of their number, a young French tailor named Martial Bourdin, into blowing up the Greenwich Observatory. Their idea was that, if he did this, the British government would hasten to round up all anarchists.

Carrying a bomb up the steep wooded slope on which the observatory sits, Bourdin was only 60 or 70 yards from it when he tripped and fell. He was blown to bits, and the observatory remained (and remains) unharmed.

Bourdin's funeral, in the Tottenham Court Road, was

attended by thousands of fellow-anarchists, mostly youthful, romantic, and harmless (which was why the British police had not even bothered to list them).

Some years later, in 1907, Joseph Conrad and some friends recalled the incident during a conversation. The conversation inspired Conrad to write his novel *The Secret Agent*, in an attempt to understand 'a blood-stained inanity of so fatuous a kind that it was impossible to fathom its origin by any reasonable or even unreasonable process of thought.' (Conrad's novel formed the basis for Alfred Hitchcock's film *Sabotage*. The title had to be changed because he'd just made a different film called *The Secret Agent*. This confuses people.)

In June 1914, Archduke Franz Ferdinand, heir to the Austro-Hungarian Emperor Franz Josef, made an official visit to Bosnia, in his capacity as commander-in-chief of the Austrian army (since 1908 Bosnia had been a province of Austro-Hungary). With him was his wife Sophia, Duchess of Hohenberg. Theirs had been a love-match, fiercely disapproved of by his uncle Franz Josef. Although she was a duchess, in the strict and snobbish world of European royalty she was not deemed sufficiently royal, so their marriage had been declared morganatic, and on most state occasions she was not permitted to accompany him. But, as he loved her dearly, on this occasion he was delighted that she could.

On Sunday, 28 June, after several enjoyable days

watching military manoeuvres, they were to attend a mayoral reception at the City Hall in Sarajevo, the capital of Bosnia. They travelled by train from Ildize, where their hotel was, and at Sarajevo entered the second of a procession of five cars. It was an open car, and sitting facing them was General Oskar Potiorek, military governor of Bosnia. In front, alongside the driver, was Count Harrach, owner of the car and head of the motor corps.

Unknown to them, there were in Sarajevo that day a number of Serbian activists, mostly in their late teens. Three, who had been smuggled in from Serbia, were members of a terrorist gang. It wanted the union of all Serbs into a Slav nation, and was officially called 'Union or Death', although it was informally known as 'The Black Hand'. The three were Nedjelko Cabrinovic, a compositor, and Trifko Grabez and Gavrilo Princip, both students. In addition, The Black Hand had co-opted three local supporters, named Mehmedbasic, Cubrilovic and Popovic. All six were armed. Four had revolvers, and each had a delayed-action bomb with a twelve-second fuse (these were to be detonated by banging the firing-cap against a hard object before being thrown). In addition, all six had been given a poison capsule for use if captured. Which was as well, because none of them was very competent, to put it mildly.

As the procession drove slowly along the Appel Quay, it first passed the three local terrorists. It passed Mehmedbasic, who had a bomb, but whose nerve failed him. He later claimed there was a policeman standing too near him. Then it passed Cubrilovic, who would have drawn his revolver except (he said) Sophia looked so pretty.

And then it passed Popovic, who also failed to shoot, claiming later that his eyesight was too poor for him to pick out the Archduke's car.

On the opposite side of the road to Popovic was Cabrinovic, the Serbian compositor, who did throw his bomb. But he wasn't good at it and the bomb landed on the furled hood at the rear of the Archduke's car. Turning, the Archduke bravely brushed it off into the road, and seconds later it exploded under the third car, severely wounding one of General Potiorek's aides.

Cabrinovic fled to the bank of the river, swallowed his poison, and jumped in. But the poison proved to be out-of-date and useless, and merely made him ill. And the river was only shallow, so he was soon hauled out by the police and arrested. The injured aide was dispatched to hospital, and the procession proceeded to the City Hall.

There the Mayor received the party, and the Archduke said to him angrily, 'We have come here to pay you a visit and bombs have been thrown at us. This is altogether an amazing indignity!'

The Mayor, shaken, somehow got through his speech of welcome, and the Archduke composed himself enough to reply, reading his prepared speech from a manuscript sprinkled with the wounded aide's blood. These formalities over, he announced that he had no intention of attending the planned lunch at General Potiorek's mansion, but instead would go to the hospital to visit the aide. Sophia insisted on going with him. If there was danger, she should be by him.

This change of plan meant that the five cars were to set off along a different route from that planned, Count

Harrach riding on the Archduke's running-board with his sword drawn. He had complained to General Potiorek that there should have been a military guard, to which Potiorek, nettled, replied, 'Do you think Sarajevo is full of assassins?'

The route was less crowded than it had been. The three local terrorists had fled. Cabrinovic was under arrest, and Grabez, unaware that the lunch had been cancelled, was waiting uselessly outside Potiorek's mansion. Only Gavrilo Princip was still on the Appel Quay, standing at the junction with Franz Josef Street. Also unaware of the change, he was waiting for the procession to make its scheduled return.

It would have turned off before it reached him, en route to the hospital, but unfortunately the drivers of the five cars had not been told of the unscheduled trip to the hospital. They headed back along the Appel Quay and mistakenly turned off it down Franz Josef Street, which was narrow. 'Not that way, you fool!' shouted Potiorek to the Archduke's driver. 'Over the bridge!' The driver braked and began engaging reverse gear.

Princip was standing right by it. He drew his pistol and fired two shots. The first hit the Archduke in the throat, severing his jugular vein, and the second, aimed at Potiorek, accidentally hit Sophia in the abdomen, severing an artery. Both wounds were quickly fatal.

The two shots were all Princip had time to fire before he was beaten to the ground by the crowd. He did, however, manage to swallow his poison. It, too, only succeeded in making him ill.

The *New York Sun*, commenting on the affair, felt that

the removal of such a strong personality would in the end make for greater peace in Europe. It didn't.

In 1941, after France surrendered to the Germans, Marx Dormoy, the former Minister of the Interior, being a leftist, was under house-arrest at a hotel in Montélimar. One evening, three right-wing activists placed under his bed a time-bomb, which later blew off his head. In placing it, they found, also under his bed, a deed-box, which they stole and took to Nice. There it too exploded, killing them. It had been another bomb, placed under Dormoy's bed earlier by co-conspirators.

15

The Criminal Mind

From the cause-driven it's almost a relief to turn to the everyday villain, whose main occupation is thievery. Which is of course in itself a sort of respect for God's creation – or at least, for certain items among it, which they wish to own and cherish. Or sometimes, admittedly, to flog down the pub for the wherewithal to fund other natural needs. They can be seen as romantic outlaws, or as resentful against a fixed and repressive society that eats at the souls of the underprivileged. But also they have a tendency, fortunate for the more law-abiding, to be somewhat weak-minded.

In May 1996 a thief sneaked into Odstock Hospital in Salisbury, Wiltshire. Wandering into various rooms, he helped himself to various bits and pieces, including several doctors' paging devices. Then he happened on a room containing a vertical sunbed. Seizing the moment, he took his clothes off and enjoyed a 45-minute suntan. Unfortunately this was not a normal domestic sunbed, but a high-voltage UV machine, and what he enjoyed was almost 300 times the recommended dose.

Hours later, covered in blisters, he was in such pain that he checked himself into the casualty department of Southampton General Hospital, 20 miles away. Staff there became suspicious because he was wearing a doctor's white coat, and soon he was arrested.

In 1982 in midtown Los Angeles, Carlos Aralijo, aged 28, decided to rob a McDonald's hamburger bar. He had the bright idea of breaking into it through a stove flue, and in the early hours of the morning he tried it. Where he wriggled feet first into the flue it measured fourteen inches square, which seemed just big enough. But what he hadn't realised was that by the time it got down to the stove it narrowed to only eight inches square.

At that point he found he could descend no further. And not only that, he was stuck. It was too greasy for him to climb out and it was dangerously hot. He began to scream for help, and screamed for several hours before he was found. Even after firefighters and paramedics arrived, it took them thirty minutes to free him, suffering from first and second degree burns to his feet and lower legs.

In 1980 in the town of Del Ray Beach, in Florida, a robber entered a bank. In time-honoured fashion he handed the cashier a note. It read, 'I got a bum. I can blow you sky height. This is a held up.' The cashier read it, burst into shrieks of laughter, and handed it to colleagues, pointing at the robber. Soon all the staff were laughing helplessly. Unnerved, the robber fled.

In New York's gangland, James Gallo and Joe Conigliaro had a problem. They felt that one of their acquaintances was a stool-pigeon. His name was Vinny Ensulo, also known as Vincent Ennisie, informally known as Vinnie Ba Ba.

On 1 November 1973 they surprised him on Brooklyn's Columbia Street and induced him to enter the back seat of a car, where James sat on one side of him and Joe on the other, each covering him with a gun. Unfortunately for them, the car, racing away from Columbia Street, suddenly swerved violently. James and Joe shot each other, and Joe, shot in the spine, was paralysed.

It became Vinny's habit after that to send Joe, every year, a present of wheelchair batteries, accompanied by a small card which always said the same thing – 'Keep rolling, from your best pal, Vinnie Ba Ba.'

What was then the greatest swindle in commercial history was carried out by Antonio (Tino) De Angelis, an ex-hog-cutter from New York City. A man in his forties, only 5 feet 5 inches in height, but weighing 290 pounds, Tino had the idea of setting himself up as a major dealer in vegetable oil.

In 1955 he formed a company called the Allied Crude Vegetable Oil Refining Corporation, and rented a tank farm in Bayonne, New Jersey. The tanks were conveniently close to the sea, and he arranged to secretly pump sea-water into them, at the same time fitting false dipping-compartments filled with a little vegetable oil. Thus he could give inspectors the impression that he was holding vast amounts of oil, and use this phantom oil as collateral in his business dealings. His entire operation was run from a single uncarpeted office adjoining the tanks.

When his deception came to light, he was found to have a deficiency of 175,927,000 short tons of oil, with a value of $62.5 million. This missing capital made it necessary for the New York Stock Exchange to close and sort itself out. This happened on 22 November 1963, at 2.07pm, and the whole affair would be better remembered if, 37 minutes earlier, President Kennedy had not been shot in Dallas.

On a summer evening in 1980 in Melbourne, Australia, things got a bit confusing. A jeweller who had his shop there entered it through a door inside the building and found a burglar attempting to escape from him through a window. Swiftly he grabbed up a rifle, dashed outside and pointed it at the burglar, making him retreat back inside.

He was still standing there, covering the window and waiting for somebody to call the police, when two men, wearing only socks and trousers, came dashing wildly round the corner. In fact they were a lover chasing a husband. The husband, who was leading, crashed into the jeweller, who was sufficiently confused to assume he was an accomplice of the burglar, and fired a shot at him, bringing him to the ground.

Instantly the lover laid into the jeweller for shooting his friend, and the two were still fighting when the police arrived. The fight was stopped, the jeweller explained that he was the shop owner, attempting to protect his stock, and the police at once mistakenly arrested both lover and husband, charging them with attempted robbery. The real burglar, meanwhile, had gone up through the building and made a clean getaway over the roof.

In 1991 the National Gallery in London was undergoing a security overhaul. For the moment it had no internal alarm system, no video cameras at the entrance, and only two warders on duty during the night. This seemed to Jason Wilkins, Martin McCracken and Philip Neasham, all men in their early twenties, like a golden opportunity to liberate a number of paintings, preferably, they thought, by Van Gogh.

To further their education, they visited the gallery. Then they drew up detailed plans of how they would rob it, and gathered a bit of equipment, including a sledge-hammer, a crowbar, some explosives, a Browning blank-firing self-loading pistol, a telescopic cosh, a survival knife, a butterfly knife, and two hand-grenades.

Planning the hoped-for disposal of the paintings, they stole a copy of *Who's Who* from a Sussex library and used it to make a list of art-collectors. Neasham and McCracken even attended a number of art lectures. They also wrote out, in hopeful readiness, cheques to Harrods for £33,000, Lloyds Insurance for £2,000 and Lamborghini for £60,000.

On the night they had in mind they drove to Soho Square (not far from the gallery) and at this point their elevated ideas suddenly descended to earth. First, they parked on a double yellow line, leaving the plans and equipment in their car. Returning after a while, they were dismayed to find they had been wheel-clamped.

This was particularly awkward because between them they had not enough money to pay the fine and get the clamp removed. So they decided to jack up the car and try to remove it themselves. At 10pm, while engaged in this illegal activity, they were spotted by police, and that was that.

Jack Drummond, aged 55, was a successful crime-writer. He was working on a new novel, entitled *Bank Robber*, in which the central character was to rob a bank in broad daylight. The twist was that he was to escape by simply walking unhurriedly away to his car in the car park, on the theory that this would disarm suspicion.

On 18 July 1978, in his home town of Columbus, Ohio, he decided to test his theory. Just after 2pm he arrived at a local bank, drove round the block a couple of times to see the lie of the land, then reversed into a park labelled 'Bank Customers and Staff Only'.

He looked carefully around to see that the coast was clear, then, for disguise (which he believed worked best if it was simple), donned a wig, a then-fashionable Zapata moustache, and heavy-framed glasses.

Unfortunately he had been spotted by a bank guard, William Nepper, who had just come on duty. Nepper saw this man park, look all round in a suspicious manner, then don a disguise. Cautiously approaching the driver's door, he demanded, 'What gives?'

Drummond, disconcerted, reached inside his coat for the toy gun he had brought as a prop. Nepper killed him with two quick shots through the brain.

It was 1976, and Billy Vecchio, of Chicago, wishing to impress his girlfriend, stole a car. But as he drove it away, it stalled. Billy hailed a passer-by and asked to be given a push. It was his bad luck that the passer-by happened to be the real owner, a man named Joe White.

Joe pointed out to Billy that the car was his, but Billy, not believing him and taking him to be some sort of wise guy, punched him on the nose. It was his further bad luck that Joe was by profession a bouncer. He broke both Billy's wrists, fractured his jaw, and then, for good measure, stabbed him. Billy died.

One night in 1969, a burglar decided to rob a New York supermarket. His chosen mode of entry was via a skylight. Making his way up to the one he had chosen, he discovered it was too small for him to squeeze through. But only just. Then he had a bright idea. If he was naked he might just manage. So he took off all his clothes and dropped them through the skylight into the store. Then he found he still couldn't make it.

In September 1979, Carlo Collodi decided to rob the Banca Agricultura in Milan. Parking his car outside, and wrapping a scarf around his face for anonymity, he sprinted into the bank, a loaded revolver in his hand.

Almost at once he tripped on the corner of a mat and fell headlong. The scarf fell from his face and he accidentally fired his revolver. Scrambling to his feet and rushing to the cashier's desk, he skidded on the beautiful marble floor and grabbed at a corner of the counter to prevent himself from falling again. This caused him to drop his gun.

By this time both staff and customers of the bank were in a state of helpless hilarity. Carlo, grabbing up his gun, turned and fled, slipping and sliding to the door across the shiny marble. Outside, he found a police officer writing him a parking ticket.

16

It's Murder Out There

Since childhood I have been fascinated by what the poet and jazz critic Charles Fox liked to call 'the English domestic murder', especially as it was during the last half of the nineteenth century and the first half of the twentieth – that era that gave rise to great public enthusiasm for its fictional counterpart, the whodunnit. But whodunnits cannot compare with the real thing. The interest of a real murder, quite apart from the excitement and drama of the act itself, lies in the detailed investigation. In no other circumstance is such a weight of research brought to bear on what, apart from the crime itself, is an unremarkable way of life. The investigations give glimpses into a secret world – the people involved, their hopes, their habits, their domestic (and often financial) arrangements, and we learn so much detail of their lives that only the most subtle and observant of novelists can hope to match it.

It was the summer of 1943, the Second World War was in progress, and Mr Brown, of Rayleigh, in Essex, was being taken for a ride in his bath-chair by his nurse, Nurse Mitchell. A man of forty-seven, he had been confined to a wheelchair for five years, his legs paralysed as the delayed result of a motorcycle accident. Even before the accident he had been known as rather a cantankerous man, and most of his cantankerousness was aimed at his wife and at his elder son, Eric, then aged nineteen and serving in the army.

Suddenly Mr Brown and his bath-chair were disintegrated by the blast of a British Hawkins No. 75 Grenade Mine. These were normally used in anti-tank warfare, but on this occasion Eric had fitted it under the seat of the chair. His sole intention, he said, was to give his mother a happier life. He was found guilty but insane. Nurse Mitchell was fortunately uninjured, though greatly surprised.

In 1947 Nina Housden set off to drive from her home in Highland Park, Michigan to Kentucky, the state she originally came from. To get there she had to cross the state of Ohio, but she had only just entered it, getting as far as Toledo, when her car broke down. A garage, after making an inspection, told her that to repair the fault would take two days.

This was inconvenient for Nina, because in the car she had her husband's body, in several pieces in several parcels. Becoming tired of him, she had strangled him, and now was on her way to dispose of his remains in the remote Kentucky hills.

She told the garage that she would stay with the car while waiting for them to repair it, and at night would sleep in it. Which she did. But while she slept a garage hand, curious about the strange smell emanating from her parcels, investigated them. Nina was arrested.

In Kansas City in 1929, a prosperous young perfume salesman named John Bennett and his wife Myrtle, after a Sunday playing golf with their friends Charles and Mayme Hofman, invited the Hofmans to their home. There, after a light supper, they all settled down to a game of bridge ('for fun stakes', as Mayme later said), family against family.

They played for some hours. At first the Bennetts won, but then they hit a run of bad luck, and began to lose. Just before midnight, Bennett dealt and opened one spade. Hofman bid three diamonds. Mrs Bennett bid three spades. Then all passed and play began.

Mrs Bennett, as dummy, laid her hand on the table, and Mr Bennett proceeded to go down by one trick. 'Well,' she said, 'of all the ridiculous plays.' This led to the pair exchanging words, and soon to Bennett making ill-bred remarks about her infertility and slapping her a few times. Mrs Bennett, upset, withdrew to their bedroom. Mr Hofman protested, and Bennett suggested perhaps it was time for the Hofmans to go home. They were tidying up to do so when Mrs Bennett came out of the bedroom holding a pistol. Her first shot hit the bathroom door. The second hit the lintel. The third hit Mr Bennett, and the fourth killed him.

Seventeen months later she was acquitted of murder, the verdict brought in being one of accidental death. It seems she had simply been bringing her husband the pistol and had stumbled, causing it to go off. It further turned out that Mr Bennett's life had been insured for $15,000, with double indemnity payable in case of accidental death. So she collected a cool $30,000.

In the south of England, in the mid-1970s, David Winder, aged 30, and his brother Thomas, aged 27, stabbed and killed Frank Ralphs, aged 31, a labourer they were giving a lift to. Then their troubles began. They felt it would be a good idea to get rid of the body, so they propped it up in the front seat of their car in a lifelike manner and drove around looking for somewhere to dump it. The first thing that went wrong was that the car broke down.

Thomas, who until recently had been in the army, phoned his mates at his old regiment, which was stationed not far away, and asked if the duty driver could turn out with a Land Rover and give them a tow. The duty driver, whose name was James Parker, obliged, and when he arrived at their car they explained to him the situation – the whole situation. Then they all discovered that his Land Rover too had broken down.

Enterprisingly, Thomas flagged down a passing police car, and asked the police in it if they would kindly give Parker a lift back to barracks. They too obliged. Parker returned with another vehicle, the car was restarted, and all three set off in it looking for a dumping-place. As they drove around they called in at Thomas's house. Where the car broke down again.

Naturally they called the Automobile Association, and while they waited for the AA man to arrive, they hid the body in the house. He arrived, fixed the fault, and left. And the two Winders and Parker set off again with the body.

This time they were more successful. They dumped the body in some woods, and repaired to a quiet nearby pub to celebrate. Getting in conversation with the landlord, they offered to show him the body, but when he went with them to the woods they discovered they'd forgotten exactly where they'd left it.

Nonetheless, that was their big mistake. After they left the pub, the landlord contacted the police. The Winders each got life and Parker got nine months for helping conceal the body.

Robert Ledru, aged 35, had worked for the Paris police for many years in various capacities (things were less structured then), and was widely respected as the most brilliant detective in France. By 1887 he was on the same salary as a Chief Inspector (and thus lived rather well), but he preferred to be known simply as 'Detective'. A tall, thin, nervous man, he had the failing of frequently driving himself to the point of collapse in his incessant desire to be the best (as he generally proved to be).

In the summer, after he had worked himself to the verge of a nervous breakdown solving a difficult case, it was decided by his superiors that he should take it easy for a while. He was to go to the port of Le Havre to investigate the disappearance of a number of sailors from nearby Saint-Addresse. The case was not deemed serious. He was to go on his own, investigate exactly as he pleased, and be in no great hurry to wind things up.

Travelling to Le Havre by train, he spent the journey reading the dossier of the case. Arriving, he discussed things with local police, visited a number of bars and questioned people who might know something, then went to bed very early in the hotel that had been booked for him. Being cautious, he put the dossier under his pillow, along with his revolver and some small valuables.

He slept deeply for twelve hours, then got up and dressed, observing with some puzzlement that his socks seemed to be damp. He decided the dampness must have been caused by the sea air.

Starting his day with a routine visit to the Le Havre police, he learned that the body of a man had been found on the beach at Saint-Addresse, naked, and presumed to have been a midnight bather. The bullet that killed him had gone right through him, and the Le Havre police were searching for it. As they were only a local force, they had asked the Paris Sûreté for help, and the Sûreté had suggested that as the great Detective Ledru was already there, he should be asked to handle the investigation. Ledru agreed.

Going to Saint-Addresse, he went straight to the scene. The police had found the bullet, and the identity of the victim. He was a Parisian shopkeeper named André Monet, aged 45, on holiday for the good of his health. His wife had been informed, and it was learned that he was not a wealthy man, and had few friends and no enemies. The clothes he had taken off to go swimming were neatly placed near his body, and had not been rifled. The only other clue the police had at all were some footprints in the sand, but even they were not much use, as they were of stockinged feet.

Ledru was shown the footprints, and at once looked perturbed. He seemed distracted, and showed no interest in questioning some rounded-up people who might have something of value to tell. Time passed, and suddenly he astonished the policeman who had been given him as an assistant by telling him he already knew the name of the murderer. Then he asked to be taken back to his hotel, and stayed in seclusion there till the next morning, when the head of the Le Havre police brought him plaster casts of the footprints, and the bullet.

The bullet, he and Ledru agreed, was from a German pistol. Ledru's pistol was German – a Luger – and it was missing from under his pillow. As was his dossier. And from the plaster casts it was clear that whoever had been on the beach in stockinged feet had a big toe missing. As Ledru had (he had lost it a few years earlier during a raid).

Returning at once to Paris, he went to see the Inspector who had put him on the case. Laying the plaster casts and the bullet on his desk, he asked to be charged with the murder (a unique instance of the detective finding himself to be the culprit). He had, he said, reconstructed what must have happened. Sleepwalking, he had put on his underwear and socks, left his room via the window carrying gun and dossier, waded round the point of the bay to Saint-Addresse (which was easy to do at low tide), seen and shot Monsieur Monet, then thrown the gun into the sea. After which he had returned the same way, still asleep, and gone back to bed.

The Inspector was disbelieving, assuming that Ledru was still suffering from nervous strain. So Ledru told him about the damp socks. He was placed in custody and, while there, closely observed. One night they left a pistol loaded with blanks under his pillow, and in his sleep he advanced towards an officer guarding him, and fired at him point-blank, next day remembering nothing.

Meanwhile the Le Havre police had found his own pistol on the beach at Saint-Addresse, along with pages from his dossier. Psychiatric experts pronounced that he was suffering from 'homicidal somnambulism'. His successful career was over, and for the rest of his long life he lived under guard in the seclusion of a farm near Paris, dying in 1937, aged 85.

In 1976, photographer Peter Hammond was taking pictures for a brochure in Takapuna, just north of Auckland. This was probably not a tourist brochure, because what he was photographing was the city dump. As he prowled round, looking for good shots, he noticed that a bulldozer, used for shifting the rubbish around and flattening it out, was approaching him.

Not wanting to interrupt the driver in his work, he stepped behind a large pile of rubbish. But the bulldozer, continuing to approach, followed him and deliberately ran him over, killing him and flattening his body into the ground. The driver, a sensitive man, later told the law he hated snoopers.

William Donoghue, a 42-year-old bus conductor, was a quiet and respectable man. He lived alone in a bed-sitting room near Waterloo Station, in London. Early one December evening in 1950 he went out to a nearby pub, the Prince Albert, for a drink. By quarter to ten he had had six or seven – all bottles of Guinness – at which time he bought a bottle of gin and headed for another pub, the Brunswick Arms.

There he met a friend, Thomas Meaney, who was 63 and worked driving a Black Maria for the police. Meaney had only had two halves of mild when they met, so Donoghue bought him another, and had another Guinness himself, generously lacing both these drinks with gin from his bottle.

When they left the Brunswick Arms at half past ten, Meaney was only a little drunk, but Donoghue was well away. He invited Meaney back to his room to have some more of the gin, and Meaney helped him there.

Once in the room, they amiably finished the gin, and then Donoghue dozed off at the table where they sat, his head leaning on it. Meanwhile, Meaney weaved his way to the bed and fell asleep on it.

Donoghue, still drunk, was wakened just before midnight by the cold, and decided to get into his bed. He had forgotten all about Meaney and, finding a figure on the bed, fuzzily assumed that some friends had put a dummy there as a joke. He dragged it off onto the floor, and it acted just like a dummy, limp and inert. Acting in the spirit of the thing, he took up a souvenir bayonet that he used as a bread knife, and stabbed the dummy repeatedly in the neck and head. The thing seemed to bleed, but that was obviously arranged as part of the joke. So he hauled it out of his room onto the landing, and went to bed.

Waking at 7.20am, he saw blood all over his floor. Puzzled, he opened his door and saw Meaney's body lying there. It was then that he began to realise what he must have done. A woman neighbour, hearing noises, looked out onto the landing, saw him standing over the body, and heard him muttering over and over, 'Is it a dummy or a body? Take it away.' He got three years for manslaughter.

Carol Hargis, aged 36, was the wife of David Hargis, a 23-year-old drill instructor in the American marines. But she had become tired of him, and decided she would be better off without him, although better off with the $25,000 she would collect from his life insurance.

In her first attempt to do away with him, she put a huge amount of the fashionable drug LSD – this was the 1970s – on his toast. But that day he wasn't hungry, and didn't eat it.

Next she packed bullets around the engine-block of his army truck, hoping that the heat would detonate them, and that one might kill him. They failed to detonate.

She thought of using a hypodermic syringe on him

while he was asleep, in the hope that air in his veins would do the job. But while she was trying it, he rolled over in bed and broke the needle.

Undaunted, she obtained tarantula spider venom, and mixed it into a blackberry pie she made him. Blackberry pie was one of David's favourite foods, but the venom discoloured the pie, and he refused to eat it, saying, 'It's gone bad, honey, but I still love your cooking.'

Her next idea was to throw a live electric toaster into his bath while he was in it, but she found out the lead wasn't long enough to reach from its plug to the bath.

So, running out of patience, she enlisted the help of a friend, 27-year-old Natha Mary Depew. Carol beat David to death with a 6½-pound sash-weight, and together they drove his body to a bridge and threw it over the side into a dried-up riverbed. Then they returned to her home and she phoned the police to report her husband missing.

Here she made her big mistake. While hanging on the phone, waiting for a senior officer to take the call, she and Natha Mary discussed alibis, unaware that as a matter of course all police calls were recorded.

Both women were arrested. At the trial, Natha Mary got off by giving evidence against Carol, who was jailed for life.

17

I'm Out of Here

Suicide has been regarded by many theologians as the ultimate sin – the rejection of all the Lord's creation – although of course nowadays there is the possible argument that on an overcrowded Planet Earth anyone who wishes to leave should be encouraged to do so. It is also, of course, one of the few actions you never regret even if it was only attempted on a passing whim. But like so many things that become your heart's desire, it can be harder to achieve than you think. Even in this driven or desperate extremity, the bony finger of failure often beckons.

In 1981 Nigel Jackson, aged 22, of Macclesfield, in Cheshire, was jilted and decided to commit suicide. After drinking seven pints of bitter, he parked outside his home, ran a length of hosepipe from the exhaust of his car into the interior, and got in. With the engine running, he settled down to see out his life with a Beatles cassette and a bottle of cider.

But before he had even passed out, the police came and tapped on his window. They accused him of being drunk and unfit in charge of a vehicle, even though he protested he had no intention of driving anywhere, but was simply trying to kill himself. He was fined £125 with £70 costs.

An American family, the Opuses – mother, father and son – was somewhat dysfunctional. Mr Opus, the father, was in the habit of threatening his wife with his shotgun, even though he himself knew it was not unloaded. Ronald Opus, the disaffected son, who did know this, secretly loaded the gun, hoping that his mother would accidentally be shot.

Six weeks passed, however, and nothing happened. So on 23 March 1994 Ronald decided his life was not worth living and he would commit suicide by leaping from the roof of the ten-storey building where their apartment was. He duly leapt, but as luck would have it, his father had at last got into such a heated argument with his mother that he grabbed the shotgun, fired it at her (no doubt being astonished that it went off), and missed. The blast, going out through a window, by an astounding fluke killed Ronald in his descent.

If it had not been for that, he would have had a good chance of surviving, because a temporary safety-net had been erected at the eighth-floor level to protect some window-washers.

Luigi Ercolli, who lived in Nardò, on the southern heel of Italy, elected to commit suicide by the desperate means of setting himself alight. In 1959 he went to a deserted headland on the coast nearby, doused himself in fuel, and lit it. But as the flames took hold, he suddenly had second thoughts, and began frantically to roll about on the grass trying to extinguish them. In doing so, he rolled over the edge and perished on the rocks below.

In 1973 John Stratton, of Manchester, had been abandoned by his wife. Depressed, he decided to kill himself. So he sealed all the doors and windows of his house, turned on the gas, and sat down to wait. Unfortunately, his house had recently been converted to North Sea Gas, which, unlike the old coal gas, is not poisonous.

He sat and waited, and as time passed he began to have second thoughts. Maybe he would give life another try after all. Turning off the gas, he took a cigar from the mantelpiece and lit it. The explosion robbed him of all further interest in continued existence. It also completely demolished the house.

Abel Ruiz, of Genoa, who had been jilted, tried to kill himself one day in 1978 by hurling himself under the Genoa-Madrid express. But he landed between the rails, and the train, passing over him, caused only minor injuries.

They were bad enough for him to go to hospital and have them attended to, which he did. But on leaving the hospital he tried to do away with himself again by throwing himself under a lorry.

Again he received only minor injuries, and back he

went to the hospital to have them attended to. By now the hospital staff were aware of what was going on, and they did their best to raise his shaken morale, allowing him to leave only after he promised not to try such a thing again. Somewhat encouraged, perhaps in part by his two lucky escapes, he did promise. But within an hour of leaving the hospital he was struck by a runaway horse and killed.

A young man living in Long Island, in New York City in the 1980s, had a quarrel with his girlfriend. It was so serious a quarrel that he became despairing and suicidal. So he ran a hot bath, got into it, and, attempting to do away with himself, dropped his video-recorder into the water. His attempt failed because he had omitted to plug it in.

Trying again, he decided to die by fire. So he set fire to the curtains in his third-floor apartment. As the fire took hold, smoke spread through the entire floor, causing a hundred residents to hurriedly evacuate it. Dragged to safety by police officers, he was charged with second-degree arson.

Henry Hey, although quite a young man (he was 31), had decided during the 1970s that his chosen career of politics was useless. Depressed, he decided to take his life by jumping off the top of the Transcendental Pyramid, which was a 300-foot high cemetery building (air-conditioned) in Tomba, Wisconsin. He duly jumped, and on his way down was heard singing 'Camptown Races'.

Miraculously, he survived, although badly injured, and, having recovered, left the hospital playing 'God Bless America' on a section of his own leg-bone, removed by the surgeons.

18

I Believe

It has become the accepted attitude, over the past hundred or so years, not to express disrespect for anyone's beliefs, whether in one god, or many gods, or an all-pervading spirit. The reason seems to be that what a person truly believes is so necessary a support for his (or her) deeply-hidden self, that to challenge it will cause him to either crumple or hit you with a brick. Respect for being themselves is what people demand. So, being at heart kindly, it is not my intention to mock belief, but simply to point out that it can be dangerous, and in unexpected ways . . .

Patrick Newell, of Vineland, New Jersey, was a high-school student. He also believed deeply in the occult. He and a number of friends used to practise satanic rites, at times sacrificing hamsters to the Devil.

One day in 1971 it came to Patrick that if he was bound hand and foot by his friends, and cast into a nearby pond, he would become a leader of demons. They obliged, but all that seemed to happen was that he drowned.

Charles Freeman and his wife Hattie lived in the small farming community of Pocasset, on the Cape Cod peninsula of Massachussetts. They had two daughters – Mildred, aged seven, and Edith, aged five, who was the pet and idol of the family.

Charles, a farmer, had in recent years become a member of the Second Advent Congregation, which was mostly made up of former Methodists. This sect was given to what used to be called 'enthusiasm', and so their meetings were extremely emotional. They believed in revelations, signs, and miracles, and they believed that Christ's personal reappearance on earth was imminent. They also believed that on death they, and they alone, would be given eternal life, while the rest of humanity would perish like soulless beasts. Charles was especially fervent, and came to believe that he would be called on to make a great sacrifice, which would result in a miracle.

In mid-April 1879 it came to him as a revelation in the night that one of his family must die by his hand. He told Hattie of his revelation, and convinced her that they should not stand in the Lord's way. He prayed long to know who was to be the victim, hoping, in his dim, honest way, that it might be himself. But a second revelation in the night told him that it was to be little Edith.

He woke Hattie and told her, and she begged him not to do it, but he earnestly entreated her not to displease God, and at length she consented. He knelt and prayed that this cup be taken from him, but his strong belief in what he had to do persisted. So he nerved himself, hoping that God would stay his hand at the last moment, as He had for Abraham. He also consoled himself with the hope that perhaps Edith would be raised from the dead in three days.

The two girls slept in one bed, and Hattie removed Mildred from it and brought her into her own bed, leaving Charles alone with Edith, and a knife. Hattie prayed for

God to stay her husband's hand, but He did not, and at 2am Charles stabbed Edith carefully in the heart. When Hattie heard the stab, she later testified, 'her heart died in her.' In mourning, she cut her hair short, stopped wearing cuffs or collars, and discarded all jewellery and articles of personal adornment.

The Lord did not resurrect Edith in three days, as Charles and Hattie had came to hope, and eventually the killing came to light. Both of them were found not guilty by reason of insanity, but their faith did not waver. As Hattie said, 'Why, if I did not believe it was ordered, what should I do? I should become insane.'

It was September 1978, and Mrs Barbara Eastman was at her job selling flowers in Naysmith Square, Toronto, when a man approached her and said, 'I am God. Could you direct me to the nearest church, please?'

Slightly taken aback, Mrs Eastman obliged. He thanked her, raising his hat, and stepped into the road where he was run down and killed by a heavy tractor. Police were never able to identify him, although he possessed an unusual tattoo – a fly, on his left buttock.

Joanna Southcott, the religious enthusiast, declared that on 19 October 1814 she would give birth to the second

Christ, whose name would be Shiloh (she would, at the time, be a 64-year-old virgin). Great preparations were made for the event by her followers (at the peak of her influence she had some 100,000), but on the appointed day Shiloh was not forthcoming. Some followers managed to convince themselves that she had truly given birth, but ethereally.

Ten days later, Joanna died, of brain-disease. She had told her followers to keep her body warm, and in three days she would rise again. Dutifully they surrounded the corpse with hot water bottles, with the result that what did happen in three days was she began to putrefy. Disappointed, they had her buried.

She left behind her a sealed box, in trust to the Bishops of England. It was to be opened only in time of national emergency, and then only by 24 bishops in conclave – not otherwise.

That was what she said, but the issue was confused by the fact that she left behind her several sealed boxes, leaving room for doubt as to which was the famous one. One, opened at the Church House, Westminster, in November 1927, in the presence of a few bishops, proved to contain an old horse-pistol, a number of coins, a dice-box, and a novel, published in 1796, called *The Surprises of Love* (probably the one by John Cleland, the author of *Fanny Hill*).

Another box, said to be at Morecambe, was reported in 1927 to contain 'a veritable old-world wardrobe, Joanna's cup and gloves and shawl . . . some curious manuscripts bearing on her visions, an address to the people of England, countersigned by George Turner, one of her followers, some "seals" conferred upon the elect of the elect, and various curious drawings illustrating her prophecies, done by Anne Underwood, and . . . the little garments prepared by her followers for Shiloh, Prince of Peace.'

The Panacea Society, based in Bedford, which continues to revere her teachings, claims that neither is the true Box. They were expecting the Apocalypse in 2000.

In 1909, in Tennessee, George Went Hensley founded the Dolley Pond Church of God with Signs Following. A fundamentalist Christian church, with a family resemblance to Pentecostalism, one of its key rituals involved snake-handling. George based this idea on Christ's promise, 'They shall take up serpents; and . . . it shall not hurt them,' (Mark 16: 18), and when he founded his church he had already been handling snakes for some ten years.

Forty-six years later, in 1955, he was still leading his church, which by then had spread through Tennessee, Kentucky, Virginia, North Carolina, Georgia, Alabama, Florida, West Virginia and California. One Sunday, at a prayer meeting in Florida, he duly handled a rattlesnake for about fifteen minutes, then attempted to put it back in its box. It bit him.

About a hundred of the congregation milled around him, praying for him, and a sheriff offered to take him to a hospital. But George refused, saying he would be saved by his faith. He wasn't.

In Astrakhan there lived a mystic, whose name was Frankel. After years of discipline his mind had reached such a high state of development that, he believed, it could stop moving vehicles by its power alone. Trying it out, he told people, he had stopped bicycles, cars, and even a streetcar. Raising his game, In 1989 he stood in front of a freight train, and willed it to stop. But his mind apparently had no effect on trains.

Joseph Smith, the son of a Vermont farmer and a devout Christian, found himself deeply troubled by the conflicting beliefs of the numerous Christian sects that were springing up in America during the mid nineteenth century. Praying for guidance, it came to him that he must found a sect of his own. Following this, he received a series of visions in which he was told of a revelation written on plates of gold (or possibly copper) and buried in a nearby hillside. These he managed to find and to translate from their 'reformed Egyptian' into English, and in 1830 he published them as the *Book of Mormon* (among many other things, it identifies the American Indians as the ten Lost Tribes of Israel).

Based on this book, he founded the Mormon religion, which attracted many adherents. Most, it must be said, were simple people with limited experience of the world. But they did not deserve to be persecuted as they were

– mobbed, beaten and shot, and driven from place to place. First establishing a community in Ohio, they were hounded from there into Missouri, and from there into Illinois. It did not help that, under Smith's leadership, they referred to themselves as The Chosen People, and to all others as Gentiles.

In 1844 their settlement in Illinois was invaded by Gentiles and Smith was murdered, thus attaining a sort of sainthood within the sect. Leadership of the sect was taken over by the energetic and ambitious Brigham Young, and soon, as their persecutions continued, he too received a revelation. The sect must all move to Salt Lake, in what became Utah, but which was then not yet a part of the United States (it belonged to Mexico). So there they went, burning their rather splendid Illinois temple behind them.

It took them two years, till 1847, to make their way to Young's newly-founded Salt Lake City. There things remained peaceful for a while. But unfortunately, in 1850, after a war between the States and Mexico ended, Mexico ceded to the States the Utah territory. So once again the Mormons found themselves in the land of the Gentiles. But as there was nobody else much living in the territory (except Indians), the Gentiles did appoint Brigham Young to be its governor.

He soon made it plain that Utah was for the Mormons, and even though the US Government appointed judges and territorial officers, the Mormons, of whom there were by now some 30,000, simply ignored them.

Some members of the sect, it is true, became disaffected and wished to leave the community. In 1857 a group of these joined a wagon-train of some hundred or so westbound emigrants who happened to be passing through.

The faithful among the Mormons took a dim view of such heresy. Brigham Young, who by now had declared himself a manifestation of God (or Great Grand Archee, who in time would rule over a heaven of his own), received a further revelation. He commanded that the wagon-train (which mostly consisted of odious Gentiles) should be pursued and all in it be slaughtered. The pursuers, led by a fanatical believer called John Doyle Lee, were to enlist the help of the local Indians (the Paiutes) and be themselves disguised as Indians.

Thus the wagon-train, by now some three hundred miles south of Salt Lake City, found itself attacked by a large party of 'Indians'. They turned their wagons into fortresses, and threw up earth mounds for defence, and managed to hold their attackers off for five days. After which time the attacking Mormons retreated, leaving a fair number of real Indians still surrounding the wagons. Having retreated, they took off their warpaint, resumed white man's clothing, and returned to the wagons bearing a flag of truce. They were greeted with cheers, and soon assured the emigrants that the local Indians were quite mad, but that they would parley with them, and then conduct the emigrants (on foot) to a nearby settlement. The male emigrants, having wives and children, agreed to this.

Soon they set off, the women and children at the front, and the men behind, escorted by thirty or forty armed Mormons, and they had gone about a mile when the Mormons opened fire on them and killed all except children of seven and under. One hundred and twenty emigrants were butchered, and the affair became famous across America as 'The Mountain Meadows Massacre'.

But, things being as they were with the law in Utah, it took 18 years before John Doyle Lee was brought to trial. And two more before he was hanged.

Mormons these days, although still enthusiastic crusaders for their religion, are fortunately more peaceable.

By the time the Mormons settled in Salt Lake City, Mormonism had spread to Britain. It was becoming fashionable in the Nottingham area, and a young man named William Barnes had recently been elevated to its priesthood. On a night in January 1852 he was to receive into the faith two new converts, both young women. The ceremony involved adult baptism, so to this end he conducted the converts and a small congregation to the banks of the river Trent, at a place known as the Rye-fields, near Beeston, at around 10pm.

The Trent was running unusually strongly at the time, and the young women were nervous about entering the water, but Barnes reassured them that no harm could come to the faithful. Then he stepped into the water to lead the way and was immediately swept away and drowned. As *The Times* commented a few days later, 'The enthusiasm of these wretched fanatics is astonishing.'

In 1885 the Roman Catholic parish church of Kildare consecrated a new altar. It was made of marble, and its tabernacle was surrounded by a spire-shaped canopy, supported on four pillars. These four pillars proceeded upwards through the canopy, and standing on each was a marble cherub weighing three stone.

In October the following year, the Very Reverend Dr J.B. Kavanagh was officiating at the seven o'clock morning mass. The service was nearing its close, and he was standing in front of the altar with his hand on the chalice when a three-stone marble cherub fell on his head. He was not expecting it.

19

Whatever Turns You On

Sex is of course wonderful. As W.C. Fields said, 'Sex may be a curse, and it may be a blessing, but one thing's for sure – there's nothing exactly like it.' For a start there is the endless variety – lovemaking can be fierce or gentle, sudden or slow, loving or angry, dominating or submissive, teasing or driving or half-asleep. But what makes it tricky is the enormous amount of emotional baggage it carries – the bonding and the togetherness, the obsessiveness, the distraction from all other concerns (and distraction can always be dangerous). No wonder those in the throes of enthusiasm sometimes find themselves in situations they are ill-equipped to handle. For all its wonderful variety, sex can prove treacherous in equally wonderful ways.

François-Félix Faure, President of the French Republic (1895–99), had worked his way up from being the son of a small Parisian furniture-maker, making his fortune in the tanneries at Le Havre and marrying well (his wife was a friend of Proust's mother).

A handsome figure of a man, he was tall, erect, and broad-shouldered. He had fair colouring, pale grey eyes, and a neatly trimmed imperial and moustache. He was intelligent, honest, and likeable, his politics were somewhere around the right wing of the left, and by early 1899 he had been President for a little over four years. He was by then fifty-nine, and of late there had been was some speculation about the state of his health. People had noticed a tendency for his pale grey eyes to become glassy, for his eyelids to be puffy, and for him occasionally to stumble over words.

On 16 February, after a stormy cabinet meeting relating to the Dreyfus affair (a major political scandal of the period), during which he stubbornly refused any revision of the case, he received, in his office in the Palais de l'Élysée, the Prince of Monaco and Cardinal Richard. During the interview they both noticed that his look was absent, and that he seemed impatient to be rid of them. After they left, he signed some decrees, and then was left alone. This was at 5pm. His office was accessible only through the office of Le Gall, the chief of the civil secretariat, and beyond his office was an elegant boudoir, decorated in blue, the last room in the presidential suite.

At about 5.30, to this office, and to this boudoir, came Madame Steinheil, a pretty, fascinating and wanton young woman, whose husband, Adolphe, was a nephew of the fashionable painter Meissonier and a portrait painter himself. She had (she said) arrived to work with the President on his memoirs. Le Gall, having admitted her, remained in his sentry-like position in his office.

At about quarter to seven, Le Gall thought he heard strange, stifled screams coming from the boudoir. After some hesitation, he forced the locked door. The President was lying unconscious, in a fit, and without his trousers. Madame Steinheil, completely naked, was kneeling by him, screaming hysterically, her hair clenched in his unconscious fist. Le Gall tried to release her, but in vain. Eventually he sent for an usher, who sent for a servant, who cut her hair from the President's grip. She dressed hurriedly and left, leaving her corset, which Le Gall kept for a souvenir. Then Madame Faure was informed, and at 7.30 a doctor was sent for. The President began to drift in and out of consciousness, but remained in a state of collapse. Eventually a priest was summoned, and at ten o'clock Félix Faure died.

The amazing Madame Steinheil went on in later years to escape being convicted of the murder of her husband (the painter) and her mother. That was in 1908, and in 1910 she moved to England, where she wrote her memoirs and, in 1917, married Robert Scarlett, fifth Baron Abinger. As the Dowager Lady Abinger, she died at Brighton in 1954, aged 85.

Wellington Smith, aged 75, was one of the leading citizens of the town of Lee, in Massachusetts. In 1910 he was President of the Smith Paper Company, which owned five large mills. He was an active Republican and personal friend of President McKinley, and he was a Deacon in the Congregational Church.

He made frequent trips to New York, usually staying at a boarding-house on 123rd Street owned by a widow, Mrs Ralph. On 26 April 1910 he arrived there with a woman named Anna. In her sixties, she was a relative of one of his business associates and not his wife, although at the boarding-house she registered as 'Mrs Smith'.

They retired to their room at half past ten, and at midnight Mrs Ralph, asleep in her room on the same floor, was gradually wakened by muffled screams. It took her some time to work out where these were coming from, but eventually she realised it was Mr Smith's room. Going to investigate, she found the door locked from the inside.

By now panic-stricken, she rushed out into the street, and happened on two young women and a young man passing by. She asked the young man if he would crawl in through the room's window and unlock the door. 'What? And be shot for a burglar? I guess not,' he replied. But one of the young women, a Miss Smallwood, was more bold. She climbed to the balcony, lowered the top sash of the unlatched window, and struggled in.

She soon unlocked the door, and all the others entered. Against the wall, folded upright into its closed position was a bed – one of those patent beds that, when closed, resembles a heavy walnut wardrobe, and which hinges down. They managed to unlatch it and lower it, and inside found Mr Smith dead with his neck broken, and Anna unconscious from suffocation. Apparently Mr Smith had not been familiar with the bed's mechanism and had not realised that its legs had to be pulled out and snapped into place. He had pulled them out only half way, with the result that the heavily-sprung bed had suddenly folded up on him and Anna.

Miss Smallwood was complimented on her bravery by everyone (except for her landlady, a few doors along, who requested both her and the other young woman to leave her house immediately as she did not care for the noto-riety).

In 1986 a four-seater Cessna light aircraft was seen flying low over the sea off Los Angeles. Watchers saw it then carry on to crash disastrously into a low hillside. Investigators, reaching the crash site found it contained only two people – the pilot, who was 57 and had held a licence for seven years, and a young woman. Tests proved that both had been over the drink limit, and as the police reported, 'By the position of the bodies and certain injuries to the pilot, the passenger was performing an act of oral sex at the moment of impact.'

Mrs Augusta Nack, a New York midwife, was a handsome, well-built woman of the voluptuous build favoured by late-Victorians. Her husband, Herman, played little part in her life. He had been the owner of a Tenth Avenue bologna shop until, as was said of him, he developed a Tenth Avenue thirst. Once he lost the shop, he lost Augusta, and to keep herself she began to take in boarders. Her first boarder, German like herself, was named Willie Guldensuppe. He worked as a rubber in a Turkish bath, and he was tall and blond, with curling moustachios and a tattoo of fruit and flowers on his chest. In no time he and his landlady were lovers.

Their affair, which began in 1894, lasted for about two years. Then Augusta's eye fell on another young immigrant, with dark curly hair and flashing black eyes.

Formerly his name had been Torzewski, but he had Americanized this to Thorn – Martin Thorn.

She transferred her affections from Willie to Martin, as she had previously from Herman to Willie. But Willie was not as accomodating as Herman had been, and objected to being cast aside. Augusta and Martin soon came to the conclusion that they had no option but to kill him. So they rented a two-storey frame house at 346 2 Street, in Woodside, Long Island, and Augusta, not mentioning Martin's involvement, invited Willie to come and inspect it.

On 25 June 1897, having got permission to take the evening and night off work at the Turkish bath, he was driven to the house by Augusta, in a surrey. They arrived at about ten or eleven at night, and Augusta asked him if he would go and have a look at the rooms upstairs while she nipped out for a moment.

Somewhat reluctantly, because he would have preferred to wait for her, he did. And waiting for him in an upstairs closet was Martin, armed with a revolver, a poisoned dagger, a bottle of carbolic acid, a hammer, a rope and a knife. He liked to be thorough.

He shot Willie three times, and Willie fell unconscious. Then he stabbed him to the heart with the poisoned dagger. When Augusta returned, they dragged him downstairs and cunningly lifted him into the bathtub before dissecting him, so that all the blood would run away down the drain. They then distributed portions of his body all around New York. Some of these were found, sure enough, and suspected of being the missing Willie, but what with the state of forensic science in those days, there was no way of proving it. Naturally suspicion fell on Augusta and Martin. Their renting of the house in Woodside came to light, and it was searched thoroughly. But not a sign of blood was found.

Alas for careful planning. It turned out that there were no sewers in Woodside. The water from the bath had run away through a nearby ditch. In this ditch swam a few ducks, and as the hot summer evaporated the water somewhat, their owner noticed that they were looking a bit seedy. Inspecting them a bit more closely, he observed that the feathers of a white one were tinged with red.

This was all the police needed. Augusta and Martin were brought to trial, and managed to be defended by the crooked and flamboyant attorney William Howe, in his last famous case. He argued with spirit, claiming not only were the remains found unidentifiable but that there never had been any such person as Willie Guldensuppe – he referred to him at various times as Gildersleeve, Goldensoup, Gludensop, Goldylocks, Silverslippers and 'a creature as imaginary as Rosencrantz's friend Guildenstern'. And he might have won if Augusta hadn't suddenly undergone a religious conversion and confessed. She got fifteen years and Martin was electrocuted.

Dr David S. Love was Assistant Professor of Anatomy at Case Western Reserve University School of Medicine, in Cleveland, Ohio. It was the 1970s, and he and his wife lived in a third-floor apartment in Cleveland Heights.

One night, seeking to add novelty to exhilaration, they decided to heighten and prolong the intensity of their love-making by engaging in a little emotional role-playing – submission, shame and fear for her; power and cruelty for him. Accordingly, he had her strip naked, tied a rope round her ankles, and dangled her upside-down outside the apartment window. At which point, as is the way of these things, he lost his grip on the rope. Falling to the ground below, she died of a ruptured liver.

Early in 1791 Susannah Hill rented rooms at 5 Vine Street, a cul-de-sac off London's Piccadilly. She had resided there for about nine months when a man came past her front door, which it was her friendly habit to leave standing open. Seeing it open, and seeing Susannah sitting invitingly in her front parlour, he engaged her in conversation and asked if she would like to have something to drink. As she had never seen the man before, she did not recognise him as the famous Czech composer, František Koczwara, creator of *The Battle of Prague*.

Being a sociable soul, she said she'd have a little porter. He said he himself would have brandy and water if she would go and get it. He gave her money to buy the porter and the brandy, and two shillings extra for some ham and beef as a snack, and she went out and bought them.

They drank and snacked, and then went into a back room where, it was later reported, 'several acts of the grossest indecency passed'. Eventually, Koczwara, finding difficulty in becoming re-aroused, suggested it might help if Susannah were to threaten to slice off his male member. For some reason she shrank from this idea, even when he reduced his request to slicing off half of it. So he further suggested it might help if he were to be hanged for five minutes. This she agreed to, although it would mean her going out again to buy some cord. As he gave her money for this further purchase, he observed that hanging would help raise his passions.

She could not find a long enough cord for sale locally, so she bought two short ones. Returning with them, she helped Koczwara to knot them together, then put one end round his neck and tied the other to the back room door. It wasn't really high enough, but by bending his knees he was able to tighten the cord against his throat.

Knees bent, he hung like that for five minutes, after which Susannah cut the cord, and to her dismay he fell forward to the floor, landing on his face and remaining as if dead. Which he was.

She ran to a local publican, who called a surgeon, who tried bleeding him, which of course proved impossible. Susannah, tried for murder, was acquitted. She had only been trying to be friendly.

In 1983 Jimmy 'The Beard' Ferrozzo, aged 40, was manager of the Condor strip club in San Francisco. His star stripper was Carol Doda, who each evening made a spectacular entrance stretched out on a gleaming white grand piano that slowly descended from the ceiling.

In the cast also was Theresa Hill, a 23-year-old topless dancer. One night in November, after work, Jimmy and Theresa took a few drinks together. One thing led to another, there was no-one else around, and they decided it would be a good thing to make love.

The site they chose was the closed lid of the white grand piano, now lowered to stage level. Its spectacular descent was made by means of a hydraulic mechanism, and while Miss Hill and Ferrozzo were engaged with each other, with the 204-pound Ferrozzo on top, somehow they tripped the switch which triggered the mechanism, and it began to rise.

Slowly, and unnoticed by them, it rose a distance of 15 feet, crushing Ferrozzo firmly against the ceiling. Miss Hill, stark naked underneath him, found herself trapped. She remained trapped for so long that eventually she fell asleep, waking hours later to find Ferrozzo still on top of her, dead from asphyxiation and growing cold. And still she could not struggle free. She became hysterical.

When they were at last found, and the fire brigade called, it took three hours to free her. Sustaining only minor bruises, she claimed she didn't even remember getting onto the piano.

20

And So It Goes

As we near the end of this parade of human fallibility, I hope that my readers will have been reinforced in the belief that we are all *fallible. Even I. For instance, here, as a sort of fanfare finish, are a set of happenings that I was totally unable to slot into any neat category. Several are among my favourites. But I console myself with the thought that even saints can make mistakes (look at St Augustine's life-corroding worry about the stolen pears). And scientists. And economists. And even politicians. Not poets, of course, at least in their work, because what they say has no need to be true. The stories in the following round-up, however, are all true. Make of them what you will.*

Norton College, in Chicago, was founded by Dr Horace Norton in the 1860s. At around that time, being a man of substance and position, he was introduced to General Ulysses S. Grant, who had recently led the Union side to victory in the American Civil War, and was soon to become President. At their meeting, the amiable Grant gave Dr Norton a cigar. Norton was so proud of this that he never smoked it, but kept it as a memento.

Seventy-five years later, in 1932, his grandson, Winstead Norton, was an honoured guest at a Norton College reunion. As such, he was expected to make a speech, and as he made it, he produced the cigar. Movingly, he told of how it had come into his grandfather's possession. Then he lit it, saying something like, 'And as I light this cigar with trembling hand it is not alone a tribute to him whom you call founder, but also to that Titan among statesmen who was never too exalted to be a friend, who was . . .' At this point the cigar exploded.

In 1822 Sir Walter Scott was rowed out in the rain to the steam yacht *Royal Sovereign*, anchored at Leith, to welcome his sovereign, George IV, who was making his first visit to Scotland. Scott was welcomed aboard, and presented the King with a silver cross of St Andrew, a tribute from the ladies of Edinburgh. Then they drank each other's health in whisky, and Sir Walter asked if he might have the King's glass as a souvenir.

He was given it, tucked it into the skirt pocket of his frock coat, and held the pocket carefully in front of him all the way home to his house at Abbotsford. There he was pleased and surprised to find that the Suffolk poet George Crabbe had arrived to visit him. In the excitement of greeting Crabbe he sat down, and immediately leapt up again with a scream and fragments of broken glass embedded in his person.

Scott didn't seem to have much luck with George IV. Ten years earlier, in 1812, when the King was still only Prince Regent, he presented to the Royal Academy an elaborate bronze lantern, weighing two tons. This they gratefully hung from the ceiling of the Great Room of Somerset House (which was then their premises). Three years later, in the middle of their Annual Dinner, which

Scott was attending, it crashed to the floor, narrowly missing him.

Philip Bourke Marston, poet and son of a poet, was blind from an early age. Although only in his thirties in the 1880s, he was bearded like an elder statesman, and had a noble and striking appearance. In 1882 he was living in a gloomy room off London's Euston Road, and minor members of the Pre-Raphaelite group would often go there to read to him.

On 3 June, James Thomson went to visit him. Thomson, notably the author of *The City of Dreadful Night*, was a greater (and older) poet, but an extreme melancholic and a heavy drinker. While with Marston, he was suddenly seized with a drunken delirium and imagined himself to be a Bengal tiger. Pouncing on Marston, who, being blind, was unable to defend himself, he mauled him rather severely.

Fortunately at this point another writer, William Sharp, arrived. Sharp was the youngest of the three and would later write mystical Celtic romances under the pen name of 'Fiona Macleod', dressing in women's clothes to do so, and insisting that Fiona Macleod had a real separate existence from himself.

Finding Thomson and Marston struggling, Sharp pulled Thomson away, at which point Thomson had a severe haemorrhage. Blood poured all over Marston, and over Sharp. Sharp ran and fetched a doctor, who, on arriving, also turned out to be drunk. He cried out that Sharp must be arrested for murder.

Eventually order was restored, although Marston almost lost his reason. Thomson, taken to University College Hospital, bled to death.

On 23 August 1981, in London, Nigerian businessman Kizito Ideheu got into a minicab driven by one Kevin Butler. He had with him a bag containing £241,000 in cash. He asked Butler to stop at a shop he wished to visit, and entered it, leaving the bag in the cab. When he emerged, cash, cab and Butler had vanished forever.

Keith J. Prager was a furrier, living and working in San Francisco. For years he had wanted to take a holiday in the South Sea Islands, and often spoke of it to his friends. They did not believe he was really serious, but in the summer of 1938, when he was 38, he figured he could afford to take six weeks off. He planned to go to Tahiti, and from there spend three weeks touring the islands. And off he went.

While in Tahiti, he learned that at that season it was possible to take a week's trip on one of the schooners that went round the smallest, least-visited islands, collecting the annual crop of copra. He was delighted by the idea, and negotiated with the half-Danish, half-Polynesian skipper of such a schooner to take him as a passenger. The skipper's name was Rasmussen, and the schooner was called the *Tiaré*. The trip was to take eight days and visit five islands.

The *Tiaré* turned out to be small and dirty, and alive with copra bugs, which bit savagely, but after 36 hours sailing it did safely arrive at the tiny island of Pounaia. There, the island's chief, Iné, regarded Prager as a VIP, and arranged for him to be entertained as such. Prager, using his school French, was able to converse haltingly with Iné and some of the other men, who spoke French a little. The beautiful Polynesian girls, even though they spoke only Polynesian, seemed disposed to regard him as a white god and, as Prager later said, it 'seemed like they were almost nearly queueing up for it.'

Rasmussen's crew loaded the copra, and in the evening after they finished there was feasting. And by next morning Prager had decided there was no need for him to travel any further. He would simply stay on Pounaia for a while. He suggested to Rasmussen that a week later, after Rasmussen had made his trip round the other islands he was to visit, he should return to Pounaia, collect Prager, and take him back to Tahiti. For a sizeable extra fee, Rasmussen agreed.

For a week, Prager had the time of his life. But then Rasmussen failed to show up. Days passed, and he began to worry about missing his boat back to the USA from Tahiti. Then he began to realise that Rasmussen had either forgotten, or wasn't going to bother, about him, and that the *Tiaré* wouldn't be back for another year. Worse, the same thought had occurred to the Pounaians, who now came to believe that he couldn't be all that important, or he wouldn't have been left behind.

The girls of course would have no more to do with him. His portions of food became small and revolting, the ethics of the tribe dictating 'no work, no food'. He tried offering money and travellers' cheques, but neither meant anything to the simple tribesmen. He attempted to work by helping with the fishing, but his clumsy splashing, which had once amused the fishermen, no longer did. He tried and failed to climb coconut palms, as he had previously done for fun, but now the natives laughed at him, not with him.

Eventually he was put to work doing the lowest and most menial jobs, mainly smashing coconut shells to separate them from the vile-smelling copra. For this he was allowed food, but only the nastiest bits of fish, and not much of that. He became so emaciated and ragged that the girls no longer bothered even to jeer at him.

After one year of this, the *Tiaré* did return, although now with a new captain and crew (Rasmussen was rumoured to have bought himself a new and better schooner). Prager was able to return to Tahiti, and thence to San Francisco. There he described his experiences as 'Hell, simple hell', but his return was rather underreported as it happened to coincide with the outbreak of the Second World War.

In 1907 Madame Magdou, a Parisienne, lost her infant son through illness. She was inconsolable. Her husband, to help her bear the loss, had the idea of putting a wax doll, dressed in the dead child's clothes, into his cradle. This seemed to help Madame Magdou. She brightened somewhat, and soon took to taking the doll for walks in her child's perambulator. One day she was wheeling the pram in Parmentier Square when it overturned, and the doll was thrown under the wheels of a passing vehicle. In her frantic efforts to save it, Madame Magdou was herself killed.

Pauline Seward, of Sefton Park, Liverpool, was a model. Her career had begun when she was 17, in 1974, but at that time she weighed only four stone and photographers told her she would look better if she put on a little weight.

As a result she began eating more, although soon it became more and more. Her career proved successful, and gradually she developed a routine where she would fast before a photo session, so as not to have a round stomach, then catch up with a huge meal, largely of vegetables, and largely raw. Her mother used to tell her, 'It's enough for four people. You could feed a family on that.' But Pauline persisted.

In 1981, when she was 24, and now weighing a healthier eight stone, she did a modelling session (after three days without eating), then came home and ate 2 raw cauliflowers, 2 whole black puddings, 1½ lb of raw liver, 2 lb of kidneys, 2 lb of raw peas, 3 lb of raw carrots, and 1 lb of mushrooms – a total of some 14 lb. Then she ate a large bag of fruit containing 10 peaches, 4 pears, 2 apples, 4 bananas, 2 lb of plums and 2 lb of grapes. Then she had some cheese with home-made bread.

Five hours later her parents found her fighting for breath in her bedroom. She was rushed to hospital, where surgeons performed an emergency operation to remove food from her swollen stomach. But they were too late. She died of gastro-enteritis.

In 1911, Bobby Leech managed to survive the daredevil feat of riding in a barrel over Niagara Falls, although he did break what was described as 'nearly every bone' in his body. Recovered, he embarked on a lecture tour round the world, to capitalise on his celebrity. In New Zealand he slipped on a banana skin, and died of complications from the fall.

One night, back in the 1950s, police in Lakeview, Ontario, were called to investigate the situation in a trailer home. In it were two men, one dead and one unconscious. The dead man turned out to be named Charles Tessier. He was covered in shaving foam. His eyes, his nose and ears were clogged with it. And in one hand he was clutching an egg.

The other man, the unconscious one, had once been a well-known jockey. His name was Frank Madeley. On his head was a salad bowl that had obviously been filled with shaving-foam. One of his arms was in a sling, a sheet had been pinned round him, and clothes-pegs were attached to his ears.

He proved to be not much help in explaining the situation, beyond admitting that he and Tessier had been drinking all day. As a baffled police officer admitted, 'All we can find out is that they must have been as drunk as they could get.'

It was during the Second World War, and a unit of the Royal Engineers was undergoing basic training in the grounds of one of Lord Glasgow's many Scottish houses. Seeing this as an opportunity, Lord Glasgow asked if they could help him. On the south side of his house was a new ten-acre larch plantation, and among the young trees was the vast unsightly stump of a dead oak, too big for his groundsmen to dig out. Perhaps the Sappers, as a sort of exercise, would like to blow it up.

The officer in charge of the unit said of course they would, and his Lordship gave him the go-ahead, only emphasising that care must be taken not to damage the trees of the new planting.

Explosives were packed into the stump, the detonating

cable was paid out to a safe distance, and the plunger was pushed home. But someone had got their calculations wrong. As the remains of the stump soared fifty feet into the air, the larch plantation was flattened, a nearby conservatory was reduced to splintered glass and rubble, and every window in the south wing of the house was blown in.

Lord Glasgow, mortified, held himself together for long enough to accept the officer's apologies, then headed for the house and hid his sorrow in the lavatory. He sat there for quite a while, until he felt he had recovered his equilibrium. Then he stood up and pulled the chain. The lavatory ceiling collapsed on him.